OUR HERITAGE

OUR HERITAGE

ESCHATOLOGICAL HOPE FOR A CHRISTIAN NATION

AUBREY JACKSON

TATE PUBLISHING
AND ENTERPRISES, LLC

Published by Tate Publishing & Enterprises, LLC
127 E. Trade Center Terrace | Mustang, Oklahoma 73064 USA
1.888.361.9473 | www.tatepublishing.com

Tate Publishing is committed to excellence in the publishing industry. The company reflects the philosophy established by the founders, based on Psalm 68:11,

"The Lord gave the word and great was the company of those who published it."

Cover design by Bill Francis Peralta
Interior design by Manolito Bastasa

Published in the United States of America

ISBN: 978-1-68352-661-2
1. Religion / Christian Theology / Eschatology
2. Religion / Christian Theology / General
16.07.05

CONTENTS

1

America Will Be Saved!

When it comes to the end-time, bad eschatology can cause people to sit silently while a holocaust comes upon them. Wrong application of scriptures can produce doubt, uncertainty, and fearful unbelief in the Body of Christ.

I'll never forget it as long as I live. Overall, the rooms were dark, with streaks of light pulsating from the stages. The celebrations were loud. The singing was always explosive. The friendliest, happiest people seemed to be all around us. Some were shouting "Praise the Lord!" and "Hallelujah!" My wife Jannie and I participated in two large Spirit-filled Church Conferences.

Nearly ten thousand people were in attendance at these major hubs of American Christian culture. This was a whirlwind week for my wife and me. First we participated in a Christian conference in Nashville, Tennessee; then we flew to Believer's conference in Tulsa, Oklahoma.

At both events there was lively and passionate praise, practical workshops, and anointed speakers. And at both conferences I experienced similar occurrences. At Nashville, a well-known fiery, miracle-working evangelist from South Africa shared how God had led him at the age of 75 to move his ministry to America. The crowd cheered and Amen-ed as he told how God had moved across Africa, saving millions of precious people.

He spoke powerfully for several minutes. Then he spoke the four words which should have been the climax of his message. As he talked about coming to America, he said: "America will be saved."

I was shocked at the response or lack of response by the crowd. Only about a third of the people in the conference center cheered politely. Had the rest not heard his words? The speaker actually said it over and over several times before getting some excitement out of the crowd of believers there in Nashville, Tennessee.

A very similar thing happened to another speaker a few days later when we were in Tulsa, Oklahoma. This charismatic speaker had a great message. The crowd adored her and hung on her every word. Then, as she began to speak of eschatology and began to say that Jesus was returning for a victorious church, the temperature in the room dropped. Faith seemed to disappear into a black hole. There were half-hearted responses among pockets of people in a crowd of nearly two thousand.

My experiences at these two conferences brought to the surface for me feelings I had been experiencing as I watched the news and talked to other Believers around me in America. As Christians, some of us really are not sure the Church can win the battles ahead. And some of us are not sure whether or not God will save America again. I was shocked at my lack of faith. But where did this unbelief come from?

As I prayed about these things, the story of Elijah and the prophets of Baal on Mount Carmel came into my mind. Look with me at the scriptures.

> And Elijah came unto all the people, and said, How long halt ye between two opinions? if the LORD be God, follow him: but if Baal, then follow him. And the people answered him not a word. (1 Kings 18:21, KJV)

Doubt and uncertainty silenced the people of God in Elijah's day. They were waiting to see what was going to happen before they cast their vote of confidence with God.

Did uncertainty gag the responses of God's people at these two Christian conferences? More importantly, will God save America this time? With so much trouble around us, how can we believe?

2
Why Eschatology Matters

There are two reference points that give life meaning: Where we come from, and where we are going. People tend to live their richest, most creative and productive lives when they understand themselves in the context of Divine history and God-ordained destiny.

My prayer in writing this book is that it will help the church in America embrace her God-ordained destiny. There are many excellent books already written about God working through the Church in the history of our country. I will leave it to you to refresh yourselves on America's Godly history. In this book we will examine scriptures that help us understand the Church's Divine destiny as a context for victory in the battles that will soon be thrust upon us by the forces of evil. As in past generations, I believe we are destined to secure freedom for America's posterity.

I believe that we are living in what the Bible calls the last days. It is important to try and follow the leading of God. In the first few years of the new millennium I felt the Lord impressing me to lead our congregation to begin prophetically declaring that America is a Christian nation.

Since that time, ungodly voices have tried to convince us all that America has entered a post-Christian era, on the way towards collapse. During this period, state and federal leadership has become progressively anti-Christian. Immorality has become rampant. The fear of terrorist attacks is increasing. And civil disobedience, murder, and other crimes are rising.

Hope is slowly being drained from my country, as more and more people are trained to believe that America is coming to the end of its life cycle as a nation. Our world is being changed by unseen forces of evil. And although some will say that our country has been through dangerous times before, this time no one seems to be talking about a brighter tomorrow.

The most popular movies, television shows, and computer games depict brutal crimes, anarchy, sexual perversions, and grotesque tortures. The only hope that seems to be offered comes from those who are in favor of some kind of global socialistic government arising after the collapse of our nation. The media seems bent on glamorizing a "post-

America world" that looks more like the "Dark Ages" in our European history books (a time when might made right, and suffering was everywhere).

There is something wrong with our thinking when hopelessness abounds. Many of the Christian leaders I listen to find their hope in the afterlife, and see no hope for this life. (There are some exceptions: Christian leaders who not only speak of hope for the afterlife, but also hope for this life, for America and all the nations of the world. To them I am very grateful.)

The God of hope wants His children to abound in hope!

> May the God of hope fill you with all joy and peace as you trust in him, so that you may overflow with hope by the power of the Holy Spirit. **(Rom. 15:13, NIV)**

The Bible is the key to all hope. Americans can recover the ability to feed themselves on the hope that God gives to us in the Bible; hope not only for the hereafter, but hope for this world as well. This Bible hope is what carried George Washington, Abraham Lincoln, and Dr. Martin Luther King, Jr. to victory in the darkest of times in our country. This hope makes us what Jesus calls the "salt of the earth."

I believe that in every undertaking or endeavor it is important to determine the goal, the end you are working towards. In other words, I believe it is important to know "the win." Understanding our purpose or goal helps us establish our priorities. So, in times like these, the ultimate question has to be: What are we living for?

Growing up, I always played in some kind of team sport: track, football, wrestling, and basketball. Although I was not a star in every sport, I liked doing whatever I could to help the team.

One of the things that being on teams showed me was that when people believe they can win (a game, a championship, or a gold medal), they are usually willing to work hard and willing to make great sacrifices in training and preparation. In other words, what we believe from the beginning about the end determines how well we set priorities and prepare.

God intended Christian Eschatology (the study of the end times) to give people hope and victory, in the darkest of times.

As I said earlier, when it comes to the end times, bad eschatology can cause a people to sit silently while a holocaust comes upon them. Wrong application of scriptures can produce doubt, uncertainty, and fearful unbelief in the Body of Christ.

Remember that Satan quoted scriptures in his temptations of our Lord Jesus Christ. And the Apostle Paul told Timothy:

> Study to shew thyself approved unto God, a workman that needeth not to be ashamed, rightly dividing the word of truth. (2 Tim. 2:15, KJV)

Think of Germany. How could the nation that brought us Martin Luther and the Reformation later bring us Adolf Hitler, the Third Reich, and the Holocaust?

In his book entitled *How Do You Kill 11 Million People?*, Andy Andrews talks about how Christians allowed Hitler's killing machine to grow.

> In at least one German town the railroad tracks ran behind the church. An eyewitness stated:
>
> We heard stories of what was happening to the Jews, but we tried to distance ourselves from it, because we felt, what could anyone do to stop it? Each Sunday morning, we would hear the train whistle blowing in the distance, then the wheels coming over the tracks. We became disturbed when we heard cries coming from the train as it passed by. We realized that it was carrying Jews like cattle in the cars!

> Week after week the whistle would blow. We dreaded to hear the sounds of those wheels because we knew that we would hear the cries of the Jews en route to a death camp. Their screams tormented us.
>
> We knew the time the train was coming and when we heard the whistle blow we began singing hymns. By the time the train came past our church, we were singing at the top of our voices. If we heard the screams, we sang more loudly and soon we heard them no more.
>
> Years have passed and no one talks about it now, but I still hear that train whistles in my sleep.[1]

After seminary, I joined the US Army. There I learned that you are more likely to defeat an enemy if you start early, convincing him that he cannot defeat you. If you keep him convinced that in the end he will not win, then he will not make the sacrifices necessary to become a winner.

A winning team or a winning army believes they will win and they prepare effectively for victory.

God describes life as a war against evil that He has predestined humanity to win. Look at some of the scriptures God uses to describe the Christian life.

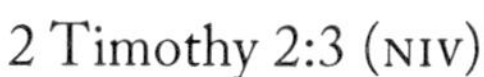

2 Timothy 2:3 (NIV):

Endure hardship with us like a good soldier of Christ Jesus.

2 Timothy 2:4 (NIV):

No one serving as a soldier gets involved in civilian affairs—he wants to please his commanding officer.

1 Corinthians 9:25–26 (NIV):

Everyone who competes in the games goes into strict training. They do it to get a crown that will not last; but we do it to get a crown that will last forever.

Therefore I do not run like a man running aimlessly; I do not fight like a man beating the air.

1 Peter 5:8 (NIV):

Be self-controlled and alert. Your enemy the devil prowls around like a roaring lion looking for someone to devour.

Ephesians 6:10–11 (NIV):

Finally, be strong in the Lord and in his mighty power.

Put on the full armor of God so that you can take your stand against the devil's schemes.

Just like a team has to believe they will win in order to make the sacrifices necessary to become winners, likewise, what we believe about the last days is important because it gives us passion to grow spiritually and do the works of Jesus. It gives us power to live with integrity for the cause of the Kingdom of Christ in the earth. It gives us endurance every day.

As a pastor I am called and anointed by God to teach people the clear scriptures about the last days (among other topics I am called to teach on), so they have a winning attitude as they go through the good and the bad in life.

I believe it is unfortunate (to say the least), that many American Christians today believe that the devil is supposed to take over the earth in the last days.

Recent polls have shown that 83 percent of Americans say that they are Christians. How is it possible for evil to flourish in our nation as it does, if 83 percent of the population is Christian? I believe that part of the reason is because the enemy has convinced Americans for generations that we cannot defeat evil.

When Christians believe that in the end the devil is supposed to defeat humanity, then they will tend to live unrestrained, self-serving, and defeated lives.

Today, I believe we live in one of the most exciting, yet dangerous times in human history. There is a day of spiritual battle coming. God wants to help us defeat the demonic forces that have kept humanity divided, sinful, and suffering. The question is, "Are we thinking victory or defeat? Do we think we can win?"

> Do not be overcome by evil, but overcome evil with good. (Rom. 12:21, NIV)

One of the lessons we learn from slavery in early American history is that in order to enslave people over multiple generations you must purposefully distort their sense of history and destiny. (In other words, you have to make them feel that their future is doomed and that they came from monkeys.)

On the other hand, when people get the proper history and destiny from the Bible, they cannot stay oppressed long. When people understand that they were created by God in His image and likeness, that they were redeemed by God from their sinful nature, and that they are empowered and destined by God to bring blessings to all the nations, families, and people groups of the earth, then their lives will become focused and effective.

This is the purpose of Biblical Eschatology. It allows people to discover from the Spirit of God who they are and why they are here on earth, at this time.

Today, when I read books about the end times, most seem to center around the events that will happen after the rapture of the church. On many end time charts there is the Cross representing the first coming of Christ and the time He spent on the earth. Then there is a blank space with a title like "Church Age." Then there is the rapture. And then after the rapture, the chart really fills up with prophecies and scriptures from Daniel, Zechariah, and Revelation.

I believe that if we are to save our nation and our world from evil, we have to focus our thinking on this age we are in. We are not responsible for what happens on earth after we are gone to Heaven in the Rapture.

We are responsible for what we allow to happen on our watch, while we are here. One man of God said, "The devil's not taking over the whole world while I'm here, because he's not taking me over!" I like that. Our eschatology needs to help us see what is possible through Christ while we are here.

Some say the church in America is in steady decline. I think we just have to get our head in the game! We just have to begin to read our Bible right, and to think right, then we will act right and save our nation!

Can we sleep at a time when our nation needs us to be the most creative and the most effective? Can we stop spreading the Gospel and building churches at a time when the institution of family is under attack, when our economy is crumbling, when our government is funding the killing of millions of innocent babies, and when our homeland is threatened by invading terrorists?

Here is another question we have to ask ourselves: What if Jesus does not come for another 59 years? What if we are wrong about the signs of the times that we are seeing? What if they are not signs of the imminent coming of the Lord? What if they are the signs of Satan trying to steal our freedom and destroy our nation like he did historically in Christian cultures throughout Africa, the Middle East, and Europe? Will we make the same mistakes other Christian have made?

What if Jesus does not come for another 1000 years? What if, when we have eaten up all our "end time food," we come out of our "end time bunkers," and we discover we have a new flag and a new constitution and Jesus did not come again?

Please don't misunderstand me. I believe that Jesus is coming. And I want to live to the fullest for Him, now and every day. But we have to ask ourselves: Have any other Christian societies ever thought that because things were bad in the culture, it meant the end of the world was near? Have there ever been other Christians who (because they thought they were all going up in the Rapture) gave control of their government, education systems, business arenas, and cultural norms over to ungodly people to rule, thinking they themselves were about to go to heaven? What happened to their children and grandchildren?

Jesus told us clearly in scriptures when he would come. It is so clear I was surprised I had missed it all these years as a Christian.

> The LORD said to my Lord, "Sit at My right hand,
> Till I make Your enemies Your footstool." (Matt. 22:44, NKJV)

Is Jesus at the right hand of the Father? Yes; the Bible tells us clearly that He is. How long will He be there? Jesus will be there, until God makes His enemies His footstool.

"Yes," you may say, "but what about the bad things that we see happening around us? What about the wars and rumors of wars Jesus talked about?"

Let's look at what Jesus said in Matthew 24:6 (NKJV): "And you will hear of wars and rumors of wars. See that you are not troubled; for all these things must come to pass, but the end is not yet."

Notice what Jesus said: "The end is not yet." Jesus tells us that there will always be wars and rumors of wars, famines, earthquakes, and pestilence, but he says, "See that you are *not troubled*."

Wars and rumor of wars happen every day.

In verse 14 Jesus gives us the true sign of the end.

> And this gospel of the kingdom will be preached in all the world as a witness to all the nations, and then the end will come. (Matt. 24:14, NKJV)

When the Gospel is spread to all nations, then the word of the Lord spoken in the Garden (Genesis 3:15) and reiterated to Abraham in Genesis 22:18 will be fulfilled, and then the end will come.

> In your seed all the nations of the earth shall be blessed.... (Gen. 22:18, NKJV)

3
The First Half

After I got out of the Army, my wife and I started a church in Radcliff, Kentucky. For over twenty years our family lived in the state of Kentucky. My wife, Jannie, did her graduate studies at the University of Alabama, and my sons, Jonathan and Joseph attended the University of Kentucky. These facts should tell you that I have watched a lot of football and basketball games over the years.

At all levels of these two American sporting events, the games are played in two halves. Each half may range from 16 minutes to 30 minutes, depending on the sport and the level of play. At the end of the first half there is a period of rest for the players before the second half begins.

Although it is true that the team with the most points at the end of the second half wins the game, the first half is also a very important part of winning. Around here, historically, some University of Kentucky basketball teams have been known as "The Comeback Cats," because although they seemed to be losing in the first half, they could come back and win in the second half of the game. Although I have been thrilled to watch many second-half comebacks, as a fan, I must admit that I prefer that the team I am cheering go into half time with a substantial lead, and then finishes off their opponent easily in the second half of the game.

Jesus Christ won the greatest victory for mankind, freeing us from condemnation to hell, and giving us power over evil in the earth. What Jesus Christ was actually doing was restoring the human race back into fellowship with God so we could again fulfill the purpose for which God made us.

> And God said, Let us make man in our image, after our likeness: and let them have dominion over the fish of the sea, and over the fowl of the air, and over the cattle, and over all the earth, and over every creeping thing that creepeth upon the earth.
>
> So God created man in his own image, in the image of God created he him; male and female created he them.
>
> And God blessed them, and God said unto them, Be fruitful, and multiply, and replenish the earth, and subdue it: and have dominion over the fish of the sea, and over the fowl of the air, and

> over every living thing that moveth upon the earth. (Gen. 1:26–28, KJV)

In verse 28 God blessed mankind (in Adam) and commanded us to "subdue the earth."To *subdue* something means to defeat, to conquer it, or to bring it back into subjection. In other words, if there was rebellion on our planet against the will of God, the human race was created in the image and likeness of God to defeat God's enemies and bring the earth back in line with the will and purposes of God.

For us to have to subdue something means that God, in His infinite wisdom, could foresee the possibility of rebellion taking place in a world of free wills. Indeed, Satan swept humanity into his rebellion, but God had prepared Jesus and His plan of salvation before the foundation of the world, to restore mankind to our original purpose.

Although everything God created was at first good, something went wrong. Something was not in compliance with the will of God. And God created the human race to subdue it. We'll talk about this more in later chapters.

As we look at what the Bible says about "end time" events, we recognize that human history is moving from Christ's victory on the cross to Christ's victory through the human race.

Someone might say, "You mean God wants to work through the church, not the through humanity." But the

Bible teaches that God's dream is that all humanity would choose to be saved and to be a part of overcoming evil in the earth. Every person is free to choose whether to follow Jesus or not. The church is made up of people who surrender to God's will for all humanity. And our numbers are growing!

As I study prophetic scriptures, I am more and more convinced that the Lord Jesus Christ is preparing the human race (those who choose to submit to and participate with Him) to defeat the spirits of anti-Christ all over the world in these last days.

I'm sure that for many, this sounds too good to be true. This may be because many Christians are like I was: unsure of the work our Lord left us to do and ignorant of the authority He gave us to accomplish that work with.

In the last 100 years, whenever we discuss the last days, American Evangelical Christians has been theologically trained to focus on the Rapture (catching away of the Church into Heaven), and the events that will happen after the Rapture. We have neglected our duty to subdue evil in culture, including government, education, business, media, and family. We have neglected our calling to defeat the devil and restore the Kingdom of God on the earth.

According to the scriptures, the last days began when Jesus came on the scene in human history (Hebrews 1:2; Acts 2:14–17). The last days can therefore be considered as the time from Jesus' first coming to the earth until the end of human history as we know it.

I suggest that when we study what the Bible says about the end times, it may help to think of the "last days" as being divided into two halves (like football or basketball). The first half consists of events that will occur before the Rapture. The second half involves the events that take place after the Church is in Heaven (events highlighted with suffering and judgments that lead up to the return of Jesus to establish His Millennium Kingdom on earth).

For many Christians, God's victory over Satan will take place largely in the second half, when Jesus returns and establishes His millennial reign on earth. But I believe it is important that we win in the first half of the war, while we are here, before the Rapture.

So what about the first half? There was a time when I was not sure we are to have victory in the first half.

What is the church supposed to do before the Rapture? Is there victory before the Millennial Reign of Christ? This book is not about the second half of the last days. It's about where we live right now, the last days, before the Rapture. It is about the first half in our war against evil.

Although we see the increase of terrorism, wickedness, and occultism all over the world, we have to ask: Has God ordained that the church sit by and let the devil take over our world? Can there be victory before the Rapture? As

I have more recently searched the Word of God, I have discovered the exciting news that God wants us to win in the first half! No matter how bad things seem, God has promised that His people will defeat the devil in the earth, before the Rapture.

4

Jesus Is Coming Back

The great joy of the Church is that Jesus, our Lord, is coming back, and believers from all over the world will be saved from what has been called the Great Tribulation.

> But I would not have you to be ignorant, brethren, concerning them which are asleep, that ye sorrow not, even as others which have no hope. For if we believe that Jesus died and rose again, even so them also which sleep in Jesus will God bring with him. For this we say unto you by the word of the Lord, that we which are alive *and* remain unto the coming of the Lord shall not prevent them which are asleep. For the Lord himself shall descend from heaven with a shout, with the voice of the archangel,

and with the trump of God: and the dead in Christ shall rise first: Then we which are alive *and* remain shall be caught up together with them in the clouds, to meet the Lord in the air: and so shall we ever be with the Lord. Wherefore comfort one another with these words. (1 Thess. 4:13–18, KJV)

But of the times and the seasons, brethren, ye have no need that I write unto you. For yourselves know perfectly that the day of the Lord so cometh as a thief in the night. For when they shall say, Peace and safety; then sudden destruction cometh upon them, as travail upon a woman with child; and they shall not escape. But ye, brethren, are not in darkness, that that day should overtake you as a thief. Ye are all the children of light, and the children of the day: we are not of the night, nor of darkness. Therefore let us not sleep, as *do* others; but let us watch and be sober. For they that sleep sleep in the night; and they that be drunken are drunken in the night. But let us, who are of the day, be sober, putting on the breastplate of faith and love; and for an helmet, the hope of salvation. For God hath not appointed us to wrath, but to obtain salvation by our Lord Jesus Christ.... (1 Thessalonians 5:1–9, KJV)

First Thessalonians and other scripture passages provide the hope that evil has been defeated and will not last forever.

First Thessalonians chapter 4 says that Christ will descend in the clouds with a shout that sounds like a trumpet from Heaven. Then the bodies of believers from all over the world will rise first. Those of us who are alive will then be caught up into the sky as well.

And we will all be changed in a moment, in the twinkling of an eye (1 Corinthians 15:51–53). Our old bodies will be transformed into glorious new bodies that will live forever!

Jesus demonstrated the powers of this new glorified body after his resurrection. One day, when the doors were shut, the disciples were gathered in hiding for fear of the Jews. Jesus suddenly appeared in the closed room with them and said, "Peace to you" (John 20:19). He could walk through walls! He later ate meals with them and eventually ascended into Heaven on the clouds. But only those who are ready when He returns will be transformed and go with him in the clouds.

In several of His parables Jesus warned that He would return and that we should all watch and be ready. In Mark 13:32–37, Jesus says that He will be like a man going away to a far country, who leaves his house, but gave authority and assigned-work to his servants. The earth obviously is his house, and people are the servants he is speaking of.

In the parable, Jesus says that we should all keep watching so that we will not be sleeping when He returns. In another parable, in Luke 19:13, Jesus says that we are to "occupy" (or do his business) until he comes. We should all be found doing the work and using the authority He gave us when He left.

In Matthew 24:14 the Master says we are to spread the Gospel to all the nations and then the end will come.

In another parable (Matthew 25), Jesus talks about faithful and unfaithful (or wicked) servants. In this parable, there were three servants, each given money by their master before he left. The two servants who multiplied what they had been given were praised as good and faithful servants and were rewarded by the master upon his return. The servant who did not multiply what was given to him was rebuked and cast away.

What has our Master left us with here on the earth? Jesus left us with the greatest treasure of all: salvation from eternal damnation in hell through the Gospel of His Grace. God loves people, and He wants every person to be saved. That is why Jesus died on the cross. We are to go into all the world and make disciples of all the nations, so multitudes can enjoy the same salvation we enjoy before the Master returns and catches all the believers up to Heaven.

Jesus gives us great insight into this "catching away" in the Gospels as well. When no one expects it, believers all over the world will be caught up into Heaven.

> But of that day and hour knoweth no *man*, no, not the angels of heaven, but my Father only. But as the days of Noe *were*, so shall also the coming of the Son of man be. For as in the days that were before the flood they were eating and drinking, marrying and giving in marriage, until the day that Noe entered into the ark, And knew not until the flood came, and took them all away; so shall also the coming of the Son of man be. Then shall two be in the field; the one shall be taken, and the other left. Two *women shall be* grinding at the mill; the one shall be taken, and the other left. Watch therefore: for ye know not what hour your Lord doth come. (Matt. 24:36–42, KJV)

From all over the world in a moment, the Body of Christ, the Church of Believers, will be raptured (caught up) to be with the Lord in Heaven. People will be standing or sitting or working side by side, and one will be taken, and the other left. When this happens, the world will be left to those who have continued to resist the message of

God's love. Evil will take over and the nations will enter what the Bible refers to as the Tribulation.

> For then shall be great tribulation, such as was not since the beginning of the world to this time, no, nor ever shall be. (Matt. 24:21, KJV)

The Book of Revelation gives us pictures of many of the events of this period.

> And I heard a voice from heaven saying unto me, Write, Blessed *are* the dead which die in the Lord from henceforth: Yea, saith the Spirit, that they may rest from their labours; and their works do follow them. And I looked, and behold a white cloud, and upon the cloud *one* sat like unto the Son of man, having on his head a golden crown, and in his hand a sharp sickle. And another angel came out of the temple, crying with a loud voice to him that sat on the cloud, Thrust in thy sickle, and reap: for the time is come for thee to reap; for the harvest of the earth is ripe. And he that sat on the cloud thrust in his sickle on the earth; and the earth was reaped. And another angel came out of the temple which is in heaven, he also having a sharp sickle. And another angel came out from the altar, which had power

> over fire; and cried with a loud cry to him that had the sharp sickle, saying, Thrust in thy sharp sickle, and gather the clusters of the vine of the earth; for her grapes are fully ripe. And the angel thrust in his sickle into the earth, and gathered the vine of the earth, and cast *it* into the great winepress of the wrath of God. (Rev.14:13–19, KJV)

After the Church is raptured from the earth, then the Anti-Christ, the Beast, and the False Prophet shall arise to deceive and take over the world. They will create a one-world government that will not last very long, but will bring great torment and suffering to every nation.

Through all of this, many people will refuse to repent, but will curse God. People will choose to give their wills to the devil, and they will suffer more and more. This continues only a short number of years as people will long for death and many will not find it under the leadership of the anti-Christ.

The nations will gather at the valley of Armageddon to destroy Israel, and take her land.

Then the Lord Jesus Christ will descend with the armies of Heaven to defeat the devil and all his armies on earth.

> And I saw heaven opened, and behold a white horse; and he that sat upon him *was* called Faithful

and True, and in righteousness he doth judge and make war. His eyes *were* as a flame of fire, and on his head *were* many crowns; and he had a name written, that no man knew, but he himself. And he *was* clothed with a vesture dipped in blood: and his name is called The Word of God. And the armies *which were* in heaven followed him upon white horses, clothed in fine linen, white and clean. And out of his mouth goeth a sharp sword, that with it he should smite the nations: and he shall rule them with a rod of iron: and he treadeth the winepress of the fierceness and wrath of Almighty God. And he hath on *his* vesture and on his thigh a name written, KING OF KINGS, AND LORD OF LORDS. And I saw an angel standing in the sun; and he cried with a loud voice, saying to all the fowls that fly in the midst of heaven, Come and gather yourselves together unto the supper of the great God; That ye may eat the flesh of kings, and the flesh of captains, and the flesh of mighty men, and the flesh of horses, and of them that sit on them, and the flesh of all *men, both* free and bond, both small and great. And I saw the beast, and the kings of the earth, and their armies, gathered together to make war against him that sat on the horse, and against his army. And the beast was taken, and with him the false prophet

> that wrought miracles before him, with which he deceived them that had received the mark of the beast, and them that worshipped his image. These both were cast alive into a lake of fire burning with brimstone. (Rev.19:11–20, KJV)

After the devil is cast into the lake of fire there will be a final judgment, and every human being whose name is not found written in the Lamb's Book of Life will be cast into the lake of fire.

Finally, the holy city, New Jerusalem will come down from Heaven. The Throne of God will move to earth, and God will abide among mankind forever. All the nations of the earth will be eternally blessed under Jesus' loving leadership.

> And he shewed me a pure river of water of life, clear as crystal, proceeding out of the throne of God and of the Lamb. In the midst of the street of it, and on either side of the river, *was there* the tree of life, which bare twelve *manner of* fruits, *and* yielded her fruit every month: and the leaves of the tree *were* for the healing of the nations. And there shall be no more curse: but the throne of God and of the Lamb shall be in it; and his servants shall serve him: And they shall see his face; and his name *shall be* in their

> foreheads. And there shall be no night there; and they need no candle, neither light of the sun; for the Lord God giveth them light: and they shall reign for ever and ever. (Rev. 22:1–5, KJV)

In the last paragraphs of the book of Revelation, Jesus promises, "Surely I come quickly."

What excitement, joy, and anticipation this wonderful promise gives us as we carry out His will on the earth.

5
When Will Jesus Return?

After Jesus rose from the dead He spent 40 days teaching His disciples about the Kingdom of God (Acts 1:3). After that He was taken up in a cloud out of their sight. As the disciples watched Jesus ascend into the heavens, two angels standing nearby spoke to them.

> And while they looked stedfastly toward heaven as he went up, behold, two men stood by them in white apparel; Which also said, Ye men of Galilee, why stand ye gazing up into heaven? this same Jesus, which is taken up from you into heaven, shall so come in like manner as ye have seen him go into heaven. (Acts 1:10–11, KJV)

The two angels affirmed that Jesus was coming back again. But where did Jesus go? And when is He coming back? These are the questions we will answer in this chapter.

When we talk about the work Jesus accomplished for our salvation, we talk about His sinless life, His crucifixion, and His resurrection. Sometimes we casually mention the ascension. I used to think of His ascension as Jesus just going to heaven to rest after doing all of His works. I didn't realize that it was actually His inauguration into the highest office of authority and power in all Creation.

Matthew, Mark, Luke, and John all record aspects of Jesus's trial before the chief priests, scribes, and elders who condemned him to be crucified. During the trial Jesus told them where He was going after his resurrection. Matthew, Mark, and Luke record his words.

> Jesus said to him, "It is as you said. Nevertheless, I say to you, hereafter you will see the Son of Man sitting at the right hand of the Power, and coming on the clouds of heaven." (Matt. 26:6, NKJV)

> Jesus said, "I am. And you will see the Son of Man sitting at the right hand of the Power, and coming with the clouds of heaven." (Mark 14:62, NKJV)

> Hereafter the Son of Man will sit on the right hand of the power of God. (Luke 22:69, NKJV)

Was Jesus making an idle threat? Was he spewing some meaningless religious references, or was Jesus describing the throne of power His Heavenly Father was about to give Him?

Before Jesus was born the angel Gabriel was sent by God to a virgin named Mary who was to be the mother of Jesus.

> Then the angel said to her, "Do not be afraid, Mary, for you have found favor with God. And behold, you will conceive in your womb and bring forth a Son, and shall call His name JESUS. He will be great, and will be called the Son of the Highest; and the Lord God will give Him the throne of His father David. (Luke 1:30–32, NKJV)

Jesus is a descendant of King David. Even before He was born the angel proclaimed that God was going to give Jesus the throne of David. In Psalm 89, David by the Holy Spirit celebrated the faithful covenant promises God had made to him.

> "I have made a covenant with My chosen, I have sworn to My servant David: 'Your seed I will establish forever, And build up your throne to all generations.'" Selah. (Ps. 89:3–4, NKJV)

> His seed also I will make to endure forever, And his throne as the days of heaven. (Ps. 89:29, NKJV):

> His seed shall endure for ever, and his throne as the sun before me. It shall be established for ever as the moon, and as a faithful witness in heaven. Selah. (Ps. 89:36–37, KJV)

God promised David that his Seed would be on His throne forever, and that his throne would be before God, as the sun in heaven.

Likewise the Prophet Isaiah spoke of Jesus hundreds of years before he was born, declaring that he would reign from the throne of David.

> For unto us a child is born, unto us a son is given: and the government shall be upon his shoulder: and his name shall be called Wonderful, Counsellor, The mighty God, The everlasting Father, The Prince of Peace. Of the increase of his government and peace there shall be no end, upon the throne of David,

> and upon his kingdom, to order it, and to establish it with judgment and with justice from henceforth even for ever. The zeal of the LORD of hosts will perform this. (Isa. 9:6–7, KJV)

As you meditate on these scriptures, consider this: Jesus did not take the throne of David at any time while he walked on the earth. When people tried to take Jesus and make Him a king by force, He escaped to a mountain alone (John 6:15).

Every Kingdom and nation has its capitol or headquarters within that nation. The capitol of the United States of America is in Washington, DC. The throne that Jesus has ascended to is not in any one city or nation on earth because God has made Him King over all nations, all cities, and all people of the earth (whether they like it or not).

> The LORD hath prepared his throne in the heavens; and his kingdom ruleth over all. (Ps. 103:19, KJV)

Sometimes, a person will say to me, "If Jesus is Lord over all the earth, why doesn't He just show Himself to everybody on the planet?" I try to explain that at first, when Jesus had risen from the dead, His disciples doubted that it was true. One day Jesus had an encounter with Thomas, one of the disciples that doubted His resurrection.

> And after eight days again his disciples were within, and Thomas with them: then came Jesus, the doors being shut, and stood in the midst, and said, Peace be unto you. Then saith he to Thomas, Reach hither thy finger, and behold my hands; and reach hither thy hand, and thrust it into my side: and be not faithless, but believing. And Thomas answered and said unto him, My Lord and my God. Jesus saith unto him, Thomas, because thou hast seen me, thou hast believed: blessed are they that have not seen, and yet have believed. (John 20:26–29, KJV)

Jesus said the greatest blessing is in believing without seeing. I realize that many people throughout history have seen our Lord with their eyes. I have not had that wonderful privilege yet. But some of those I have heard of said they were completely overwhelmed by His majesty.

One missionary told of a night when Jesus came into his room, and the missionary lay on the floor for some time, unable to move or stop weeping in the presence of Jesus. Look at what happened to John when he saw the glorified Lord on the isle of Patmos:

> And when I saw him, I fell at his feet as dead. And he laid his right hand upon me, saying unto me, Fear not… (Rev. 1:17, KJV)

John too was overwhelmed by Jesus's glory. There will come a time when everyone will see the glorified Jesus, and at that time every knee shall bow (whether they want to or not). At that time, every creature, every demon, and every person will confess that He is Lord, not out of love, but because they will not be able to resist His power, His glory, and His majesty.

Until that time, I believe God wants every human being to hear the Gospel so they have the chance to love Jesus by choice (because He first loved us). During this season of grace (before the Rapture), God wants every person, every family, every city, and every nation to choose to submit to the Lordship of Jesus by faith, so they can receive His bountiful blessings.

Jesus declared that he would ascend to take the throne after His resurrection. It is important to understand that according to the Bible, Jesus did not just "go to Heaven" like the rest of us do when believers die. After Jesus rose from the dead and after He spent forty days talking with His disciples about the Kingdom of God, He ascended in the clouds to sit on David's Throne of power, with God Almighty, in Heaven.

> And while they looked steadfastly toward heaven as he went up, behold, two men stood by them in white apparel; Which also said, Ye men of Galilee,

> why stand ye gazing up into heaven? this same Jesus, which is taken up from you into heaven, shall so come in like manner as ye have seen him go into heaven. (Acts 1:10–11, KJV)

The two angels that spoke to the disciples right after Jesus ascended in the clouds said that He was coming back. But when is He coming back? There has been much speculation about when Jesus Christ will return. Many have tried to set dates and give predictions. But the Bible itself tells us clearly when Jesus will return. Several scriptures all say the same thing:

Psalm 110:1 (KJV):

The LORD said unto my Lord, Sit thou at my right hand, until I make thine enemies thy footstool.

Matthew 22:44 (KJV):

The LORD said unto my Lord, Sit thou on my right hand, till I make thine enemies thy footstool?

Acts 2:34–35 (KJV):

For David is not ascended into the heavens: but he saith himself, The LORD said unto my Lord, Sit thou on my right hand, Until I make thy foes thy footstool.

1 Corinthians 15:25 (KJV):

For he must reign, till he hath put all enemies under his feet.

Hebrews 10:12–13 (KJV):

But this man, after he had offered one sacrifice for sins for ever, sat down on the right hand of God; From henceforth expecting till his enemies be made his footstool.

These prophetic scriptures are not obscure. You do not need a special revelation to understand them. They are clear and they all agree. Jesus Christ will not return to the earth until *after* His enemies have been made His footstool.

I used to think Jesus is resting in Heaven, waiting for evil to take over the world so he could come back, defeat Satan, rescue us, and reign on the earth. But I was wrong. It is clear in the Bible that Jesus will return *after* His Kingdom has subdued his enemies on the earth.

On top of all of this, here is another important fact: Jesus does not have to come back to earth to defeat the devil. According to the New Testament, Jesus has already defeated the devil!

Colossians 2:15 (KJV):

And having spoiled principalities and powers, he made a shew of them openly, triumphing over them in it.

Revelation 1:18 (KJV):

I am he that liveth, and was dead; and, behold, I am alive for evermore, Amen; and have the keys of hell and of death.

1 John 3:8 (KJV):

For this purpose the Son of God was manifested, that he might destroy the works of the devil.

By dying on the cross and rising from the dead, Jesus defeated Satan and every other demon once and for all. He fought and defeated the hoards of demons that held humanity in bondage to sin and to fear. Jesus took the keys of death and hell. He spoiled, disarmed, defeated, and stripped all demonic forces and made an open display of his triumph over them. In short, Jesus destroyed the works of the devil forever.

Jesus is not resting in heaven. He is reigning from the throne of David over all the earth. He is increasing God's government and peace throughout the earth. Think of how Christianity has grown in human history. It began with our Lord Jesus himself, one man, spreading the love of the Heavenly Father, in a small part of the world, 2000 years ago.

Today, Christianity is by far the world's largest religion, with an estimated 2.2 billion adherents, nearly a third (31 percent) of all 6.9 billion people on earth.

The Lord Jesus Christ is advancing God's kingdom, not with bombs and torture, but with miracles and love. Jesus is Lord, and He is reigning now. And He will continue to do so, from His throne until the devil and all of his demons are made His footstool and the nations are filled with God's love and blessings.

In Matthew 16:18–19 (KJV), Jesus tells Peter and the rest of His disciples: Upon this rock I will build my church; and the gates of hell shall not prevail against it. And I will give unto thee the keys of the kingdom of heaven: and whatsoever thou shalt bind on earth shall be bound in heaven: and whatsoever thou shalt loose on earth shall be loosed in heaven.

Jesus didn't build a church while He walked the earth. Today, He is building churches all over the world from His throne in Heaven.

When John the Baptist came announcing who Jesus was, he declared that Jesus was going to baptize people in the power of the Holy Spirit, the power to do the miracles of God, heal the sick, and cast out devils.

"I indeed have baptized you with water: but he shall baptize you with the Holy Ghost" (Mark 1:8, KJV).

Yet, Jesus never baptized one person with the Holy Spirit while he walked on the earth. Jesus did promise that when He ascended to the throne, He would send back the Holy Spirit.

"Nevertheless I tell you the truth; It is expedient for you that I go away: for if I go not away, the Comforter will not come unto you; but if I depart, I will send him unto you" (John 16:7, KJV).

In Acts chapter 2, after Jesus was seated on his throne in Heaven, the disciples were gathered together in Jerusalem waiting for the promised power of the Holy Spirit.

When Jesus sent the power of God upon them there was a loud noise from Heaven. The disciples began to celebrate because of what Jesus was doing. People around town came rushing to see what had happened. Peter stood and prophetically announced what had just occurred.

> Men and brethren, let me speak freely to you of the patriarch David, that he is both dead and buried, and his tomb is with us to this day. Therefore, being a prophet, and knowing that God had sworn with an oath to him that of the fruit of his body, according to the flesh, He would raise up the Christ to sit on his throne, he, foreseeing this, spoke concerning the resurrection of the Christ, that His soul was not left in Hades, nor did His flesh see corruption. This Jesus God has raised up, of which we are all witnesses. Therefore being exalted to the right hand of God, and having received from the Father the promise of the Holy Spirit, He poured out this

> which you now see and hear. For David did not ascend into the heavens, but he says himself: 'The LORD said to my Lord, "Sit at My right hand, Till I make Your enemies Your footstool."'

The Lord Jesus Christ had made it to the Throne of His father David in Heaven and was now empowering the human race to defeat the curse and to put the devil under our feet.

As you read on in the Book of Acts you see more of Jesus's activities as He began spreading His Kingdom on earth from His throne in Heaven. Jesus knocked Saul of Tarsus to the ground and temporarily blinded him (Acts 9:1–8). Jesus commanded one of his followers to go lay hands on Saul so he could regain his sight (Acts 9:10–18). Jesus sent an angel and broke Peter out of prison (Acts 12:1–11). Jesus spoke to the Apostle Paul, commanding him to speak boldly and assuring Paul that He was with him (Acts 18:9, 10).

Jesus ascended to the throne of God's power in order to empower His Church to defeat the gates of hell and put the devil under our feet. Throughout the Book of Acts, the Apostles understood this and they allowed God to use them against the forces of evil everywhere.

Jesus told those who condemned him to die that after his death, He (the Son of man) was going to sit at the right hand of God's power. In other words, Jesus was going to be the one with all power, and the one dispensing the power of God from Heaven to His Church. When He rose from the dead, Jesus was going to reconnect humanity (those who choose to follow Him) with the power of God to defeat evil.

"But from now on the Son of Man will be seated in the place of power at God's right hand" (Luke 22:69, NLT).

In Luke 22:69, the word *power* is translated from the Greek word *dynamis*. It is the root from which we get our word "dynamite." It means ability, might, miracle, strength, and power.

After his resurrection Jesus proclaimed the same thing to his disciples.

> And Jesus came and spake unto them, saying, All power is given unto me in heaven and in earth. (Matt. 28:18, KJV)

> Jesus approached and, breaking the silence, said to them, All authority (all power of rule) in heaven and on earth has been given to Me. (Matt. 28:18, AMP)

In Matthew 28:18 the word for *power* is the Greek word meaning *delegated authority* to rule and command.

Think of what this means: Jesus is not just in heaven. He is on the right hand of God, and He has been given power and authority to rule and command things not only in heaven but also on earth. God's enemies have already been expelled from heaven (Revelation 12:7–9). Now, Jesus has power and authority to subdue all demonic forces on earth. And he is delegating His power to people so they can defeat the devil, like He did.

"Most assuredly, I say to you, he who believes in Me, the works that I do he will do also; and greater works than these he will do, because I go to My Father" (John 14:12, NKJV).

Jesus went to the throne of David in Heaven so He could empower us to do the works that he did on the earth.

> Behold! I have given you authority and power to trample upon serpents and scorpions, and [physical and mental strength and ability] over all the power that the enemy [possesses]; and nothing shall in any way harm you. (Luke 10:19, AMP)

> Then cometh the end, when he shall have delivered up the kingdom to God, even the Father; when he shall have put down all rule and all authority and power. For he must reign, till he hath put all enemies under his feet. (1 Cor. 15:24, 25)

Even in these last days, the Lord Jesus Christ is making God's power and presence available to anyone who will make Him the Boss of their life. Jesus will work with us from Heaven today, just like He did with the early Church in the Book of Acts. And we will subdue the devil before we are taken up in the rapture. We will win the nations to Christ. We will have ever increasing revival, peace, love, and prosperity all over the world until Jesus comes. We will bring the will of God and the Kingdom of God to all people groups on earth, and take them to Heaven with us when we go.

Is there opposition? Yes. There is organized, well funded, collaborative, international demon-inspired opposition to God, just as there has always been in human history. Christian nations have fallen before. Whole continents have been plunged into darkness. Historically, the devil has won some battles. But we should not let our losses and our failures discourage us. The Lord Jesus Christ is perfect. He has risen from the dead. He has already defeated death, sin, and Satan. That guarantees that if we don't give up, with Christ's help, we can defeat the devil also, no matter what the odds.

> And these signs will follow those who believe: In My name they will cast out demons; they will speak with new tongues; they will take up serpents; and if they drink anything deadly, it will by no means hurt them; they will lay hands on the sick, and they will recover. So then, after the Lord had spoken to them,

> He was received up into heaven, and sat down at the right hand of God. And they went out and preached everywhere, *the Lord working with them* and confirming the word through the accompanying signs. Amen. (Mark 16:17–20, NKJV, emphasis added)

One of the most important prophecies about Jesus's second coming is found in the Psalms. This prophecy is repeated over and over in the New Testament, yet for so long I never considered it when studying end time prophecies.

"The LORD said to my Lord, 'Sit at My right hand, Till I make Your enemies Your footstool.'"

While many speculate about the time of Jesus's return, and the signs of His coming, Psalm 110:1 tells us clearly and specifically when Jesus will come from heaven, and what is to happen while he in heaven.

"The LORD said to my Lord, 'Sit at My right hand, Till I make Your enemies Your footstool'" (Ps. 110:1, NKJV).

Jesus has been made King of heaven and earth by God Himself to empower His new, born again human race to put the devil and all the forces of darkness under our feet. When we recognize who Jesus is, and what He is capable of doing through us, then we give ourselves to Him and allow Him to use us to fulfill the Father's will. The Church (this new humanity) is destined to overthrow evil in the earth. Through them all nations are to be blessed in the earth.

> Therefore, being a prophet, and knowing that God had sworn with an oath to him that of the fruit of his body, according to the flesh, He would raise up the Christ to sit on his throne, he, foreseeing this, spoke concerning the resurrection of the Christ, that His soul was not left in Hades, nor did His flesh see corruption. This Jesus God has raised up, of which we are all witnesses. Therefore being exalted to the right hand of God, and having received from the Father the promise of the Holy Spirit, He poured out this which you now see and hear. For David did not ascend into the heavens, but he says himself: "The LORD said to my Lord, 'Sit at My right hand, till I make Your enemies Your footstool.' Therefore let all the house of Israel know assuredly that God has made this Jesus, whom you crucified, both Lord and Christ." (Acts 2:30–36, NKJV)

The Bible tells us clearly how long Jesus will stay in heaven: until his enemies are made his footstool.

The Bible tells us clearly when Jesus will return for us in the Rapture: when his enemies have been made his footstool.

The Bible tells us clearly what is going to be happening on earth before the Rapture: God is working through us, making his enemies his footstool.

6
Inauguration of the King

While many are looking for another great event in the future, I think it is important to remember that the greatest event in human history has already occurred. It was when Jesus came to the earth (born of a virgin), lived a sinless life, died for our sins, rose from the dead, and ascended to the throne of David at the Heavenly Father's right side. A man with flesh and bones was seated on the throne with God!

> "But of that day and hour no one knows, not even the angels in heaven, nor the Son, but only the Father. Take heed, watch and pray; for you do not know when the time is. It is like a man going to a far country, who left his house and gave authority to his servants, and to each his work, and commanded

> the doorkeeper to watch. Watch therefore, for you do not know when the master of the house is coming—in the evening, at midnight, at the crowing of the rooster, or in the morning—lest, coming suddenly, he find you sleeping. And what I say to you, I say to all: Watch!" (Mark 13:32–37, NKJV)

Of course the Lord's coming in the Rapture is something we all look forward to. The Bible makes it clear that one day Jesus is going to come in the clouds and catch all the believers away suddenly into heaven, from all over the world.

> For the Lord Himself will descend from heaven with a shout, with the voice of an archangel, and with the trumpet of God. And the dead in Christ will rise first. Then we who are alive and remain shall be caught up together with them in the clouds to meet the Lord in the air. And thus we shall always be with the Lord. (1 Thess. 4:16–17, NKJV)

Over and over in the Gospels, Jesus tells believers to watch for that day. Notice what he says in Mark 13:34 (KJV): For the Son of man is as a man taking a far journey, who left his house, and gave authority to his servants, and to every man his work, and commanded the porter to watch.

When I was in elementary and preschool my two younger brothers and I would sometimes be left with a babysitter when our parents went out for a few hours alone. We really loved those times, because that was when we would wrestle and "shot at" each other like on TV. Among our favorite toys, we had some plastic alphabets. They were about an inch tall. Each was yellow, red, blue or green. And they had a small magnet on the back to attach magnetically to a metal board. These letters were to help us learn our ABCs (before computers).

For us, these harmless alphabets were our "bullets" to throw at each other after watching The Lone Ranger, Roy Rogers, Combat, or the Man from U.N.C.L.E. on TV.

We played out all kinds of scenarios when our parents were gone. Each projectile was an imaginary bullet. We were "shooting" at each other, ducking and dodging "bullets" and then fighting all over the room, just like we saw on our favorite TV shows.

It didn't take long for us to start getting into trouble when our parents came home, for throwing things in the house. They would find toys on the floor where we had left them.

Over time, we learned to make sure we watched for when our parents might be coming home. Someone had to look out of the window periodically, to see if their car was backing into the driveway. (To me this was a very important task. Because there was so much at stake, I seldom would assign lookout to either of my younger brothers. I did the lookout myself!)

We lived on the side of a mountain in West Virginia, so our parents had a lot of stairs to climb to get from the driveway to our house. Once we sighted them, we would scramble trying to put away every toy before they came into the house.

Sometimes we would see them backing the car into the garage. This gave us more time to pick things up. Some days we would see them opening the gate and starting to climb the stairs. Some days we would see them passing the window, about to step onto the porch. Most of the time we didn't see them until they stepped into the door!

Faithfulness is something children learn eventually. At first, you have to watch them all the time to get them to do what you want them to do. If parents are gone for a short time, children will play. Could we, as God's children, be looking for signs of the Rapture because we have not learned to live faithful lives for Christ?

Sometimes it seems like my Christian friends and I are like children waiting for "parent-Jesus" to come back in the Rapture. We are watching the signs. Why? So we won't get caught playing instead of doing what we are supposed to be doing.

In Mark 13, Jesus is describing the plan of salvation, and it is important to see these events in the context of God's plan. Jesus is telling his disciples that he is going to leave them. Why is Jesus leaving them? Because that is the plan of God.

When he leaves them, where is he going? He is going ultimately to a throne, a seat of authority and power. (When Jesus tells a similar parable in Luke 19, He says that a certain nobleman went into a far country to receive for himself a kingdom, and to return.)

When he went, what did he leave for them? "*Who left his house, and gave authority to his servants, and to every man his work.*" When Jesus ascended to heaven, he left for humanity authority and work. Why? That was the plan of God. Too often Christians are looking for the rest and rewards of heaven, but they are unaware of the authority and the work they have been given on earth.

> Watch therefore, for you do not know when the master of the house is coming—in the evening, at midnight, at the crowing of the rooster, or in the morning—lest, coming suddenly, he find you sleeping. (Mark 13:35–36, NKJV)

Basically the Lord is telling us that we should never stop using our authority and doing our work in the earth.

> And the Lord said, "Who then is that faithful and wise steward, whom his master will make ruler over

> his household, to give them their portion of food in due season? Blessed is that servant whom his master will find so doing when he comes. Truly, I say to you that he will make him ruler over all that he has. But if that servant says in his heart, 'My master is delaying his coming,' and begins to beat the male and female servants, and to eat and drink and be drunk, the master of that servant will come on a day when he is not looking for him, and at an hour when he is not aware, and will cut him in two and appoint him his portion with the unbelievers. And that servant who knew his master's will, and did not prepare himself or do according to his will, shall be beaten with many stripes. (Luke 12:42–47, NKJV)

Here Jesus is expressing the same thought. It is the unfaithful servant who is constantly looking to see when the Lord is coming so he can "appear to be working" when the Master shows up. What God wants is for the church to get the revelation of the authority and work that He has made available to us, so that when Jesus returns he finds us doing what he told us to do.

When Jesus came to the earth the first time it was to liberate the human race from the powers of the devil. By paying for our sins, giving us his righteousness, teaching us how to pray, and leaving us the Holy Spirit, Jesus equipped the human race to do what we were originally created to do: subdue evil in the earth (Genesis 1:28).

Jesus gave the human race authority and work so we could fulfill our destiny. Our future, our destiny is the same thing God promised in our history (God declares and describes the end from the beginning—Isaiah 46:10; Isaiah 48:5).

Jesus came to fulfill the promise God made to Satan in Genesis 3:15 (NKJV), the day that Adam and Eve walked away from God in the Garden: "And I will put enmity Between you [Satan] and the woman, And between your seed and her Seed; He shall bruise your head, And you shall bruise His heel."

Jesus didn't stay on the earth because that was not God's plan. God's plan was for Jesus to die and empower mankind, to destroy the works of the devil and to make earth like heaven.

In Jesus's parable in Mark 13, the householder left his house and went away on a far journey.

Jesus is talking about himself. Where did He go? He went to heaven. I was amazed when the Lord showed me this revelation about His position in heaven.

In a parable recorded in Luke 19 Jesus gives us more information about His leaving the earth.

> Therefore He said: "A certain nobleman went into a far country to receive for himself a kingdom and to return. So he called ten of his servants, delivered to them ten minas, and said to them, 'Do business till I come.'" (Luke 19:12–13, NKJV)

In this parable it is said that the nobleman was destined to return. Until he returned, he left his servants to carry on his business. In this parable, the nobleman went away to receive for himself a kingdom. Again Jesus is talking about Himself in this parable.

Jesus didn't just go to heaven (like my mother and grandmother are in heaven today). Jesus went to heaven and received a Kingdom. He ascended to the throne of David and he was inaugurated as King of heaven and earth, by the heavenly Father Himself.

That is why Jesus said in Matthew 28:18–19 (NKJV): "All authority has been given to Me in heaven and on earth. Go therefore and make disciples of all the nations, baptizing them in the name of the Father and of the Son and of the Holy Spirit."

Ask yourself, "Why does Jesus need power and authority over the earth, while he is in heaven?" (My mother and grandmother are in heaven and they have no power over the earth!) Here is what I have discovered: Jesus has been given authority over the heaven and earth so that he can delegate that authority and power to human beings, empowering us to overthrow forces of darkness in the earth. Why? Because that is the plan of God.

7

The Earth Is the Lord's: A Last Days Parable

Once there was a man who was very good and kind. He traveled a lot in his work. In his travels from city to city, he found a place that he really loved and decided that when he stopped traveling in about ten years, he was going to settle down and live in that place. So, he built himself a huge state-of-the-art home. Everything in the home was just like he liked it. He built the kitchen just like he liked it. He built the rooms just like he liked them. He had all the most modern features and appliances for comfort and enjoyment put into this new home.

Soon, it came time for him to travel again. He decided to lease his home out, so he started looking for someone to lease the house and take care of it while he was away. He found another family, who loved everything about the house, just as much as he did. So he leased it to them, and they promised to take good care of it until he returned.

Things went very well for the first year. Then, late one night, while everyone was asleep in the house, there was a knock at the door. The husband went down to see who it was. He yelled through the door, "Who is it?"

The reply came, "I have a gift."

"What sort of gift?" he asked.

"Something that will make your life in this house much better," came the reply.

When the man opened the door, several people rushed in, beat him, and took over the house. Year after year, these evil people ran the house and the leasers and all their children were their slaves. The invaders brought many large animals to live in the house and made the poor family take care of them. In a short period of time, the house was ruined. The walls had huge holes broken in them. The carpets and furniture were destroyed. None of the appliances worked liked they were designed to. After four years, the family that had leased the home all became sickly and frail because of their captors' mistreatment.

One day the son of the enslaved family was sent to town to get the mail. And a gift came from the owner of the house to their family. He sent them weapons, supplies, and a note with a plan by which they could defeat the evil invaders. The family followed the plan and liberated themselves from the invaders.

Once they were free, they continued to live in the house and to defend it from invaders, until their lease ran out and the owner returned to retire in his home.

When the owner returned he asked the family who had loved the house as much as he had, if they would continue to live with him in the house for the rest of their lives. They were overjoyed because they loved the man and the house, but they felt badly that they not taken very good care of the house, and that now it was nothing like it was when the owner had built it.

So the owner left the house for a short while and this time he took the family with him, while he had the house totally recreated. When they returned every remnant of evil was gone from the house. Every wall was new. The appliances were new. The carpet was new. Everything was new and they all liked the new house even better than they did the first house. So they all lived there together, happily ever after.

That house represents our earth. God not only wants the souls He created, He also wants the creation He created. God told the children of Israel to get the gold and silver from Egypt before they left. The Bible says the meek shall inherit the earth (not the skies).

Mankind was created for the earth. We were created to subdue evil and spread God's Kingdom on the earth. This is our house. We have let the devil bring his mess up in our house! And God wants to help us clean up the mess.

In the end, the book of Revelations shows us that we will come back to live eternally on the earth with God. That means that the earth has been and may always be our responsibility under God. If the earth is the Lord's, He certainly does not intend to let the devil have it.

This is how some Christians think: God created man in His image and told them to subdue the earth. They couldn't do it. Satan defeated them. Jesus came to pay for their sin and to get them out of the earth. Then one day God will have to come back Himself and defeat Satan because the ones God created and said would defeat Satan couldn't do it.

If that were the way the story ends, Satan would appear to have stopped God's plan. We know that can never be the case!

It is through mankind that evil will be subdued in the earth, men and women submitted to the Lord Jesus Christ will defeat the devil and bless the nations before the Lord returns to reward us for our work. Only after the church is gone is evil supposed to take over the earth. Then judgments and wrath will be poured out on the earth by God. The earth will burn with fervent heat, and all those left behind with the devil will go into the lake of fire. Then God will create a new Heaven and a new Earth wherein dwells righteousness.

The Bible makes it clear that God does not lie, what He said from the beginning will come to pass.

Something is going to happen before Jesus gets up from His throne and returns in the clouds to rapture the church. Regenerated human beings, a new species of mankind (humble, forgiven, born again, and empowered by God's Presence) will subdue evil and release God's blessing over all the nations. Then the end will come.

> Seek him that maketh the seven stars and Orion, and turneth the shadow of death into the morning, and maketh the day dark with night: that calleth for the waters of the sea, and poureth them out upon the face of the earth: The LORD is his name: That strengtheneth the spoiled against the strong, so that the spoiled shall come against the fortress. (Amos 5:8–9, KJV)

Jesus told us to pray, "Your kingdom come. Your will be done on earth as it is in heaven" (Matt. 6:10, NKJV)

Surely He wants us to keep making the world we live in better, as long as we are here.

Surely He is with us to give us solutions to problems that Satan is causing in our world. If we as Christians give up on the world, who will Jesus have to work through?

It is clear we are living in the Last Days. And according to the Bible the Last Days began with the outpouring of the Holy Spirit at Pentecost.

> But Peter, standing up with the eleven, raised his voice and said to them, "Men of Judea and all who dwell in Jerusalem, let this be known to you, and heed my words. For these are not drunk, as you suppose, since it is only the third hour of the day. But this is what was spoken by the prophet Joel: 'And it shall come to pass in the last days,' says God, 'that I will pour out of My Spirit on all flesh; Your sons and your daughters shall prophesy, Your young men shall see visions, Your old men shall dream dreams. And on My menservants and on My maidservants I will pour out My Spirit in those days; And they shall prophesy. I will show wonders in heaven above and signs in the earth beneath: Blood and fire and vapor of smoke. The sun shall be turned into darkness, and the moon into blood, before the coming of the great and awesome day of the LORD. And it shall come to pass that whoever calls on the name of the LORD shall be saved.' (Acts 2:14–21, NKJV)

Joel had prophesied hundreds of years earlier that God would pour out His Holy Spirit on humanity in the last days. When Jesus ascended to the throne of power in Heaven, He sent the power of God, signifying that the Last Days had begun.

This was the same Holy Spirit that He himself had been filled with, so that He could do miracles.

> How God anointed Jesus of Nazareth with the Holy Spirit and with power, who went about doing good and healing all who were oppressed by the devil, for God was with Him. (Acts 10:38, NKJV)

Notice what Jesus told his disciples about the Holy Spirit in Matthew 12:28 (NKJV): "But if I cast out demons by the Spirit of God, surely the kingdom of God has come upon you."

Jesus cast out devils and healed the sick by the power of the Holy Spirit. Throughout his ministry Jesus modeled for us all what a people with God's presence and power could do against Satan's Kingdom. He went about liberating people who were bound by the works of the devil. For centuries Satan has spoiled humanity. But now Jesus, our champion, has freed us and given us power to storm the gates of hell on earth, liberating our brothers and sisters from sin and leading our world back from the brink of destruction.

In the Last Days, Jesus is making the power of God available to all humanity from His throne at the right hand of God in heaven, and Satan is working through deception to keep us feeling helpless and afraid.

But we are not helpless. And we are learning to resist the spirit of fear.

Yes, we live in dangerous times. Yes, uncertainty and even hopelessness abound. Yes, evil is rising like we have never seen before. Yet God has not left us helpless.

In these Last Days He is pouring out His Holy Spirit upon people, young and old, of every race, culture, and background. The purpose is clear: so together, mankind can put evil under our feet.

Certainly there are some in our country today who are already resigned to a future dominated by foreign powers and oppression. We are being fed these thoughts over and over through the media. The good news is that God seldom starts with a majority. (Sometimes He can't get many people to believe Him!)

God starts with one or two, or twelve. He starts with a David or a Jonathan, a Deborah, a Gideon, a Moses, or twelve disciples. But eventually people rally to the good. People awaken to the will of God. They follow the few who are following God. If you have come this far in this book I believe you are one of the ones Jesus will use to ignite a movement, a revival that will save our country.

Through Jesus, we can stand and defeat Satan's attempts to destroy our nation and our planet. Together, we can do what we are destined to do, what we were created to do: overcome evil in our house (America).

> Finally, my brethren, be strong in the Lord and in the power of His might. Put on the whole armor of God, that you may be able to stand against the wiles of the devil. For we do not wrestle against flesh and blood, but against principalities, against powers, against the rulers of the darkness of this age, against spiritual hosts of wickedness in the heavenly places. Therefore take up the whole armor of God, that you may be able to withstand in the evil day, and having done all, to stand. (Eph. 6:10–13, NKJV)

8
Sonship and the Father's Plan

And if you are Christ's, then you are Abraham's seed, and heirs according to the promise.

—Galatians 3:29 (NKJV)

The power to fulfill our destiny is revealed more and more as we embrace our identity, who the Bible says we are.

One day a woman came to Jesus because her daughter was possessed with a devil. Because she was not a Jew, Jesus told her that it was not right to take the children's bread and to give it to the little dogs.

The woman responded, "This is true, Lord, but even the dogs eat from the crumbs that fall from their masters' table." Jesus commended her for her faith and healed her daughter (Matthew 15:21–28).

In this encounter, Jesus reveals to us the importance of identity. It's important to understand that the blessings of God belong to the children of God.

The key to getting answers to our prayers is first to know whether the thing we are praying for is God's will for us (I John 5:14, 15). Then, in Mark 11:22, Jesus tells us that when we pray we are to, "Have faith in God." You cannot really have faith that in the end God will help you obtain something that you have no right to claim.

God wants every person "born again" and growing spiritually, so we can resist the devil and posses the fullness of all God has prepared for humanity.

> But as many as received him, to them gave he power to become the sons of God, even to them that believe on his name. (John 1:12, KJV)

Jesus came to give people a new birth and a new way of thinking.

Let me try to illustrate my point this way. Let's say that you, the reader, and I, the writer, were very good friends. Maybe we live in different parts of the country, yet we manage to meet with our families at least once a year to catch up on old times. Suppose that my father was a very wealthy man and he left a great fortune to his children. (This is just make-believe!)

When it is time for the reading of the will, the children would be named and their inheritances apportioned. If you were present, upon hearing of my new fortune, you would be happy for me, but you would not expect your name to be mentioned when it is time to receive part of the inheritance. Why? You are not in the family. You are not one of the children.

But if (in our illustration), my father had adopted you, and named you in his will, guess what? Your name would be listed with the rest of the family. There would be an inheritance for you. We would be celebrating your fortune because the blessings of the father belong to all the children. Being in the family makes the difference.

Look at this glorious revelation from the book of Ephesians 1:3–11 (NKJV): Blessed be the God and Father of our Lord Jesus Christ, who has blessed us with every spiritual blessing in the heavenly places in Christ, just as He chose us in Him before the foundation of the world, that we should be holy and without blame before Him in love, having predestined us to adoption as sons by Jesus Christ to Himself, according to the good pleasure of His will, to the praise of the glory of His grace, by which He has made us accepted in the Beloved. In Him we have redemption through His blood, the forgiveness of sins, according to the riches of His grace which He made to abound toward us in all wisdom and prudence, having made known to us the mystery of His will, according to His good pleasure which He purposed in Himself, that in the dispensation of the fullness of the times He might gather together in one all things in Christ, both which are in heaven and which are on earth—in Him. In Him also we have obtained an inheritance, being predestined according to the purpose of Him who works all things according to the counsel of His will.

These scriptures tell us that it was always the plan of God to bring humanity into relationship with Him and into inheritance, by adoption through Jesus Christ.

John 1:12 says that to those who receive Jesus, he gives power to become the sons of God.

One day the Lord showed me that even though I was a Christian, I still was not thinking like a dog under the table. Then the Holy Spirit led me to two scriptures He used to change my thinking.

> Let this mind be in you, which was also in Christ Jesus. (Phil. 2:5, KJV)

> The Father loveth the Son, and hath given all things into his hand. (John 3:35, KJV)

I started saying them over and over to myself, "Let this mind be in you, which was also in Christ Jesus: the Father loveth the Son, and hath given all things into his hand."

First John 3:1–2 (KJV) says, "Behold, what manner of love the Father hath bestowed upon us, that we should be called the sons of God: therefore the world knoweth us not, because it knew him not. Beloved, now are we the sons of God, and it doth not yet appear what we shall be: but we know that, when he shall appear, we shall be like him; for we shall see him as he is."

When God originally created mankind, He created Adam as His son to subdue evil in the earth (see Luke 3:38). When Adam and Eve joined Satan's rebellion, they walked away from the family of God. Jesus said the human race became children of the devil (John 8:44).

God sent Jesus to bring His children back into His family, back into our inheritance, and back into our responsibility. But instead of thinking like Sons, the church seems to be hiding under the table.

Could it be that we don't know who we really are, what we really have, what we can really do, where we came from and where we should be going?

In Numbers 13 and 14 is the story of when the nation of Israel was about to enter the Promised Land. Moses sent 12 spies to look over the land before they attacked it.

Two of the spies came back with a good report and joyfully proclaimed that Israel could take the land with God's help.

Ten of the spies came back and said, "Yes, the land is good, but there are giants in the land with walled cities. We are like grasshoppers compared to them. We are like grasshoppers in our own eyes. We cannot go up against them."

The whole nation believed the 10 spies and instead of going into the Promised Land with God, they wandered in the wilderness another 40 years until most of them died.

How we think determines how we act. Wrong thinking can cause us to miss the plan and will of God.

In the media today people talk about the decline of America. There is a feeling of hopelessness hovering over our nation. Some people think it is because these are the last days. But could it be that we are just being deceived in our thinking? What if God is not finished with America? What if God wants to help us put poverty, racism, adultery, abortion, perversion, and terrorism under our feet?

God sent Jesus to make us Sons and Daughters so we could think, pray, and act like Sons and Daughters in the Heavenly Father's family. This is why Jesus taught us to pray, "Our Father…Thy Kingdom come. Thy will be done in earth as it is in Heaven."

In prayer meeting after prayer meeting, Christians are "repenting for the sins of America." However, the Lord could be calling the church to repent, not for the world's sins, but for our way of thinking.

In Matthew 4:17, Jesus says, "Repent: for the Kingdom of Heaven is at hand."

Repent is a Bible word that has confused us in the past. We thought the word repent means "feel sorry," or "make yourself better." But really the word *repent* means to change the way you think. *Re*—go back to. *Pent*—the high place. (Think of words like *pent*-house.) It literally means to go back to the higher way of thinking. Jesus's way of thinking is much higher than ours. Jesus always thinks victory. He never thinks defeat.

In Matthew 4:17, Jesus says, "Repent (go back to God's higher way of thinking)." Why? Because the Kingdom of Heaven is accessible to those who think the way God thinks.

In Isaiah 55, God says: "For My thoughts are not your thoughts, nor are your ways My ways," says the LORD (Isa. 55:8, NKJV)"

"Let the wicked forsake his way, And the unrighteous man his thoughts; Let him return to the LORD, And He will have mercy on him; And to our God, For He will abundantly pardon" (Isa. 55:7, NKJV).

Maybe God is saying that the repentance He is looking for from the church is for us to come from under the table, and begin to think according to the new identity Jesus Christ has made available for the human race.

> Therefore, if anyone is in Christ, he is a new creation; old things have passed away; behold, all things have become new. (2 Cor. 5:17, NKJV)

Can we defeat evil in the last days? Can we bring heaven's solutions to the myriad of complex problems facing our planet? Can we bring industry and prosperity back to our nation? Can we see the nations of the world delivered from poverty, terrorism, and colonialism through the Gospel? Can we end pornography, sex trafficking, and slavery? Can we put the devil under our feet before we get raptured out of the earth? I think we can, if we begin to think like Jesus.

> Let this mind be in you which was also in Christ Jesus. (Philip. 2:5, NKJV)

When a person gets born again the Holy Spirit will help them learn to think like the Son.

Philippians 2:5 begins with the word *let*. *Let* means "yield to," "permit," "allow," "make way for." When you are born again, God wants you to let, yield to, permit, allow, and make way for the mind of Jesus (the firstborn Son) to be in you.

If the church began to think like the Son, could we stay under the table when the world needs us so much?

> The Father loves the Son, and has given all things into His hand. (John 3:35, NKJV)

Would we be thinking about getting out of the world or bringing the Kingdom of Heaven into the world?

Would we be praying together for ways to defeat the devil, or would we be sitting in a bunker, thinking about how the devil is defeating us in the last days?

One day, Jesus was asleep in the back of a boat. There came a great storm on the sea, and the disciples were afraid the boat was sinking. When they woke Jesus up, he calmed the storm and the sea with one command. When the disciples saw that the sea and the storm obeyed Jesus, they were in awe. They said to one another, "What kind of man is this?"

Identity—who we are, or at least who we believe we are—affects what we do. Before Jesus returns, God says the church will put the devil under our feet. To do that is going to call for a higher way of thinking. We have to begin to think in line with the Word of God.

First John 4:17 says, "As he is, so are we in this world."

> But when the fullness of the time had come, God sent forth His Son, born of a woman, born under the law, to redeem those who were under the law, that we might receive the adoption as sons. And because

> you are sons, God has sent forth the Spirit of His Son into your hearts, crying out, "Abba, Father!" Therefore you are no longer a slave but a son, and if a son, then an heir of God through Christ. (Gal. 4:4–7, NKJV)

One of the things we have inherited as sons and daughters of God is "duty." As our big brother, the Lord Jesus said, "I must be about my Father's business" (Luke 2:49).

9
Postmillennial Eschatology

One of the most important theological shifts among American Protestant Evangelical Churches occurred after WWI, when many Christians were moved from a postmillennial eschatological position to a premillennial eschatology.

Eschatology is the study of what the Bible says about the end times, and is an important part of the systematic theology studies of seminarians and Bible School students, who will later become pastors and teachers of the Church. Periodically teaching and preaching on eschatology helps provide meaning and impetus for Christians as they do their best to carry out the commission of Christ in their lifetime.

I believe there is what I call *Biblical Eschatology* and what I call *Bad Eschatology*. Biblical Eschatology studies the promises of God's Word and gives courage and hope to people concerning the last days. Bad eschatology is the doctrine of devils which misuses scriptures to cause people to be confused and docile in the face of evil.

Premillennialism believes that the world is doomed to get worse and worse until Jesus returns. In premillennialism it is Christ's return that brings about Kingdom change in the world.

Postmillennialism is the belief that Jesus will return after the Gospel dominates the earth by the power of the Holy Spirit working through the Church. Postmillennialism teaches that the proclaiming of the Gospel of Jesus Christ will win untold masses of human beings to salvation across the earth. This increasing success of Christ's love will gradually produce a time (before Jesus returns) in which salvation, peace, righteousness, prosperity, joy, and love will prevail in the affairs of people and of nations, through the Gospel.

The postmillennial understanding of scripture can be found in the writings of Church leaders such as John Wesley. Dr. Vic Reasoner wrote an article called "The Hope of a Christian World: Wesleyan Eschatology and Cultural Transformation."

In his article, Dr. Reasoner writes:

> In his sermon "Scriptural Christianity," John Wesley connected the pentecostal work of the Spirit in

apostolic days with the great end time climax of the church.

But shall we not see greater things than these? Yea, greater than have been yet from the beginning of the world? Can Satan cause the truth of God to fail? Or his promises to be of none effect? If not, the time will come when Christianity will prevail over all, and cover the earth. Let us stand a little, and survey this strange sight, a Christian world.

Wesley then quoted Isaiah 2:2–4, Isaiah 11:6–12, and Romans 11:25–26 as primary descriptions of that Christian world. He preached,

Against hope believe in hope. It is your Father's good pleasure yet to renew the face of the earth. Surely all these things shall come to an end, and the inhabitants of the earth shall learn righteousness. "Nation shall not lift up sword against nation, neither shall they know war any more." "The mountain of the Lord's house shall be established in the top of the mountains;" and all the kingdoms of the world shall become the kingdoms of our God. "They shall not" then "hurt or destroy in all his holy mountain."

Wesley expressed the hope that the Methodist revival would not die. "No; I trust this is only the beginning of a far greater work—the dawn of "the latter day glory."[2]

Nineteenth century social reforms in America including the abolition of slavery were inspired by Christians with a postmillennial eschatology, who believed that the Gospel was given to mankind to make the world better through Jesus Christ's Spirit and His love.

Today's popular premillennial eschatology (the belief that the world can only get darker, and worse until Jesus returns) began to be systematized by Edward Irving, in 1825. Irving spread his eschatology to Scotland in 1828 and 1829. It was later made popular in America by J. N. Darby and C. I. Scofield. The 1909 publican of the *Scofield Reference Bible* with his reference notes gave the premillennial eschatology widespread popularity.

Until WWI postmillennialism was the predominant view of the evangelical Christian landscape in America.

Stephen Douglas Wilson, from Paducah, KY, a former member of the Southern Baptist Convention Executive Committee, wrote an article called, "FIRST-PERSON: WWI's impact on Christians."

Stephen Douglas writes:

> The war and its destruction marked the beginning of a fundamental shift in the Christian worldview. After the war and over time, Christians felt less positive about their standing in the world and began to express some pessimism about world affairs. The

> war launched a new interest in "end of time prophecy" that peaked in the latter half of the 20th century as the new millennium neared.[3]

Later in the same article, Mr. Douglas continues:

> As the horrors of World War I unfolded and uncertainty set in after the conflict, many Christians began to question the idea that human society would get better. Therefore, the First World War marked the beginning of postmillennialism's decline. Some still adhered to it after the conflict, but a Second World War, the holocaust and a Cold War with the threat of nuclear destruction led most Western Christians to abandon postmillennialism.
>
> ...While the First World War began to discredit postmillennialism, the war gave new impetus to a premillennial view of the end times popularized earlier by John Nelson Darby and C.I. Scofield. Premillennialists rejected the belief that the world would get better before Christ returned. They saw in the war proof that human society without Christ was in fact getting worse. Pessimistic about human affairs, they believed that Christ would return soon to redeem the elect from an evil world.[4]

I think it is instructive to note that what changed the eschatological view of 20th century Protestant America was the dark circumstances of the age in which they lived. According to some authors, Americans became skilled at "newspaper exegesis," in which they interpreted the Bible using current events.[5]

I bring this up because I believe that America is in danger, and that the Gospel of Jesus Christ is the only remedy for the challenges we face in the 21st century. I believe Satan is intentionally spewing fear and pessimism through our media, arts, and entertainment to cause Americans not to effectively resist evil.

People do right when they believe right. To believe that the world is doomed and cannot get better is contrary to John 3:17 (KJV) and Matthew 16:18 (KJV) where Jesus said, "For God sent not his Son into the world to condemn the world; but that the world through him might be saved." "Upon this rock I will build my church; and the gates of hell shall not prevail against it."

Regardless of what challenges face us in the near future, we must keep the faith, the hope, and the love of the Gospel. As I said earlier, a team or an army that believes they can only lose has lost before the games or the battle begins. Jesus is not a loser. We are following the ultimate winner. Jesus has already defeated the devil, and He has given us power to overcome evil with good on earth.

I believe that Christians are ready to spread the Gospel, give, vote, run for offices, serve, and do whatever it takes to save our nation from the devil. But they need to be reminded from the pulpit that God is Almighty; that Jesus is Lord of all Heaven and earth; that the Holy Spirit is with us; that the Word of God is more powerful than the lies of the devil; that we are supposed to win!

People need to be taught that, according to the clear, overwhelming witness of scriptures, the Lord Jesus Christ is risen and seated on the throne in Heaven. And He will remain seated, dispensing Holy Ghost power and directives to the Church, from the right hand of God, until after the devil is made His footstool and all the nations of the earth are blessed.

10
Good Kings and Bad Kings

As we have said, many Christians in America are pessimistic about the future. They have been made to believe that things are supposed to get increasingly more evil until Jesus comes. The bottom line is that many Christians believe that it is God's will that humanity suffer under Satan's rule until Jesus comes back and rescues us.

But where did we get that idea? We have already examined the ascendancy of premillennial eschatology among Protestant Evangelicals in American history, but the question still remains, "Why?"

The Jesus Movement was a revival happening among young Americans in the late 1960s and the 1970s. The movement began on the west coast among hippies and swept across the nation particularly on college campuses.

Although I grew up in church, I encountered the Jesus Movement on my college campus.

Jesus became very real to many of us who had grown up in church. Jesus and his love gave meaning and context to life. He gave purpose for school, purpose for family, purpose for society. The world needed love and Jesus had love for the world.

Many young adults were genuinely saved and committed to Christ during those years. Revival was flourishing from coast to coast. Thousands were born again and filled with God's Holy Spirit.

Here is the question: Why are those former young college students not leading our nation in godliness today? Why are abortion and sexual perversion the national policies of America today? Why are divorce, false religions, witchcraft, paganism, humanism, evolution, and other evils dominating our nation?

Jesus told his disciples that the Kingdom of Heaven was made up of children. (Matthew 19:13–15). In other words, Jesus was saying that children are very important to the Kingdom of Heaven on earth. Jesus thought in terms of successive generations. He knew that Kingdom advances could be lost in a generation. What Jesus was saying is that the Kingdom must be successfully passed from generation to generation in order to sustain victory over the devil.

One teaching that was prevalent among the Jesus Movement was premillennial eschatology. Prophecy teachers, with their books about the doom of planet earth, became very popular. Many in the Jesus Movement believed that the end was near, Jesus was coming in their lifetime, and that it was not possible to improve the world. The mission of these young Christians became to get themselves and everyone else ready to be saved out of the world before it collapsed into the hands of the devil.

As these young Christians became older, they never made the connection between the Kingdom of God and the culture. They became pastors and church leaders and kept their passion for Jesus focused on individual evangelism. They seldom thought of discipling nations as the transformation of culture. They continued to reject the world, and to wait for Jesus's return. They could not imagine the Kingdom of God making society substantially more Christian, because they believed society was destined to get worse.

These maturing Jesus-people took their pessimistic view of culture into their roles in family, government, education, entertainment, business, where ever. Meanwhile, humanity was hungry for hope. These Christians left a huge vision vacuum into which the devil quickly maneuvered ungodly leaders with their own brand of hope and their own agenda for America.

> But the Lord said unto him, Go thy way: for he is a chosen vessel unto me, to bear my name before the Gentiles, and kings, and the children of Israel. (Acts 9:15, KJV)

In Acts 9:15, Jesus Christ spoke from Heaven to a disciple named Ananias about God's plans for Saul of Tarsus. Jesus told Ananias to go lay hands on Saul because God had chosen Saul to carry Jesus's name before three groups of people: the Gentiles, the children of Israel, and kings. Kings are very important in God's plan. Saul, who became the Apostle Paul, encouraged Timothy to pray for kings and all in authority (1 Timothy 2:1–2). And in the Bible, there are good kings and there are bad kings.

King Agrippa was almost persuaded to be a Christian (Acts 26:28). King Herod killed James, the brother of John, and planned to kill Peter. (Acts 12:1–11).

> And the nations of them which are saved shall walk in the light of it: and the kings of the earth do bring their glory and honour into it. (Rev. 21:24, KJV)

> Why do the heathen rage, and the people imagine a vain thing? The kings of the earth set themselves, and the rulers take counsel together, against the LORD, and against his anointed, *saying*, Let us break

> their bands asunder, and cast away their cords from us. (Ps. 2:1–3, KJV)

In the Bible, kings are people of influence and power. Kings are leaders. As I said, there are good kings and bad kings. Revelation 21:24 and Psalm 2 represent the difference between good and bad kings (good leaders and bad leaders). Good leaders (good kings) bring the glory and honor of their kingdoms under the Lordship of Jesus Christ, God's Son.

Bad leaders (bad kings) work to free culture from the influence of God, making polices against Christianity and laws that separate the Lord Jesus from culture.

Because the Christians retreated into their churches, today, we have people in leadership (bad kings), all over America, who want to break away from under God and who oppose the Church of Jesus Christ. They (knowingly or unknowingly) follow Satan's vision for a unified world without national boundaries and without God.

Satan has been working since the Tower of Babel to enslave humanity under his demonic rule. Throughout history, God has used different languages and the sovereignty of nations to keep Satan from covering the world with poverty, plagues, suffering, and despotism. Through ungodly rulers, Satan has tried to conquer the world. Time and time again, God has rescued a remnant of people, and they

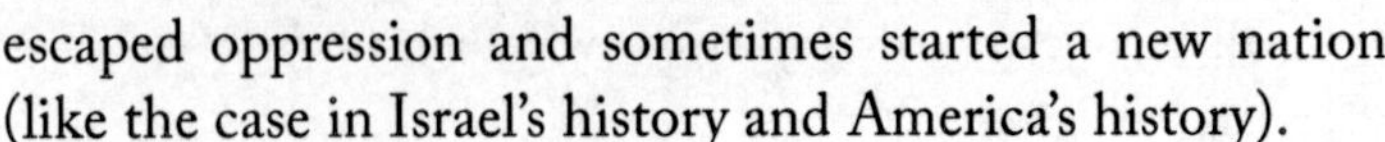

escaped oppression and sometimes started a new nation (like the case in Israel's history and America's history).

Let me ask you an important question before we go any further. Did any American banks help fund Adolf Hitler and the Third Reich?

The BBC reported in 1999:

> A French government commission, investigating the seizure of Jewish bank accounts during the Second World War, says five American banks Chase Manhattan, J.P Morgan, Guaranty Trust Co. of New York, Bank of the City of New York and American Express had taken part.
>
> It says their Paris branches handed over to the Nazi occupiers about one-hundred such accounts.
>
> ...Documents reveal that Brown Brothers Harriman (BBH), acted as a US base for the German industrialist, Fritz Thyssen, who helped finance Hitler in the 1930s before falling out with him at the end of the decade.
>
> ...The New York-based Union Banking Corporation (UBC)...represented Thyssen's US interests....

By the late 1930s, Brown Brothers Harriman, which claimed to be the world's largest private investment bank, and UBC had bought and shipped millions of dollars of gold, fuel, steel, coal and US treasury bonds to Germany, both feeding and financing Hitler's build-up to war. [6]

So there were major US banks that supported Adolf Hitler. This is important because it helps us realize that, historically, there have been some very wealthy, very influential Americans who have worked diligently against US sovereignty and for Satan's vision of a one-world government without national boundaries and without God. These "bad kings" and their families have been covertly working Satan's plan for years.

In his book, *Cheque Mate, The Game of Princes*, Dr. Jeffrey A. Baker writes:

> Those who would establish the new World Order are at the bottom line pragmatic…If it means that they have to destroy a system which they have built, which we call communism, and replace it by the same system using another name with a slightly different look, they will do it. If they have to destroy the economy of the United States to bring about their world hegemony, they will do it. To them, as pragmatists, **the end does justify the means…** The end, or course, is to establish a New World Order, which concentrates economic, political and "religious" hegemony and control of that hegemony in their hands.[7]

Dr. Baker outlines the history of certain organizations involved in efforts to weaken the United States from within. He lists their plan of attack which includes "abolition of a sense of patriotism and nationalistic intent," "abolition of... any sense of ownership in private property through societal collectivism," "abolition of family, family life, and the institution of marriage...," and "the abolition of religion—specifically Christianity." [8]

Dr. Baker goes on to point out that:

> This cadre of secret world government proponents began making remarkable penetration into the power structures of the American press. They were able to accomplish this through their influence over five American newspapers. These papers included *The New York Times, New York Herald Tribune, Christian Science Monitor, The Washington Post,* and the *Boston Evening Transcript.*
>
> Because they used their money and influence to their shrewd advantage, the shadowy members of this secret society have been hiding behind their front organizations such as the Council on Foreign Relations and have dictated American foreign and economic policies, and many aspects of life in America...their influence, if not outright con-

> trol, has extended from the Ivy League to media (including the national television networks); from governors' mansions of many states to the halls of Congress; and even to 1600 Pennsylvania Avenue.[9]

The reason things are getting more frightening, more wicked, and more dangerous in our country is not because it's the end of the world. (However, there are those with great influence who want us to think that it is.) In fact, according to Dr. Baker, these very rich people practice controlling the way masses of people think.

Do you remember Y2K? By the time New Year came around in 2000, leaders (kings), in government, businesses, media, educational institutions, and even some religious organizations had spread the notion of a world collapse due to computers not being able to turn from 1999 to 2000 in their counters and calendars.

This group of very rich anti-Americans practice using the media to produce fear, chaos, and division in our country. Through these people, Satan holds control of all three branches of our federal government (the Judicial Branch, the Legislative Branch, and the Executive Branch). And the devil is infiltrating the church with pessimism, unbelief, and shortsighted doctrines that keep the church from being effective against wickedness in America.

In spite of all of this, Psalm 118:24 says that the good news is that "this is the day that the Lord has made, we will rejoice and be glad in it!"

In other words, this is the day to go possess the promise of God by faith, and when we do we will enter into God's rest.

> But exhort one another daily, while it is called To day; lest any of you be hardened through the deceitfulness of sin. For we are made partakers of Christ, if we hold the beginning of our confidence steadfast unto the end; While it is said, Today if ye will hear his voice, harden not your hearts, as in the provocation. For some, when they had heard, did provoke: howbeit not all that came out of Egypt by Moses. But with whom was he grieved forty years? *was it* not with them that had sinned, whose carcases fell in the wilderness? And to whom sware he that they should not enter into his rest, but to them that believed not? So we see that they could not enter in because of unbelief. (Heb. 3:13–19, KJV)

God has victory for us in this life, before the rapture and before the second coming of Christ. Christ's first coming was enough to give us power over the devil, but we have to put our faith in His Word and begin obeying His voice. Today is the day to fight the good fight of faith, for America.

You may ask, "If Jesus gives us rest (Matt. 11:28), why do we need to fight?" Friend, it is because there are demons who challenge your right to rest. Hoards of demons all over the world have come to steal, kill, and destroy (John 10:10). The peace that God gives comes as we obey Him and subdue our enemies, as we put the devil under our feet.

1 Kings 5:4 (KJV):

But now the LORD my God hath given me rest on every side, *so that there is* neither adversary nor evil occurrent.

1 Chronicles 22:18 (KJV):

Is not the LORD your God with you? and hath he *not* given you rest on every side? for he hath given the inhabitants of the land into mine hand; and the land is subdued before the LORD, and before his people.

2 Chronicles 14:7 (KJV):

Therefore he said unto Judah, Let us build these cities, and make about *them* walls, and towers, gates, and bars, *while* the land *is* yet before us; because we have sought the LORD our God, we have sought *him*, and he hath given us rest on every side. So they built and prospered.

The rest that God gives in the Bible comes as we subdue the demonic forces arrayed against humanity.

Psalm 110:1–2 (KJV):

The LORD said unto my Lord, Sit thou at my right hand, until I make thine enemies thy footstool. The LORD shall send the rod of thy strength out of Zion: rule thou in the midst of thine enemies.

Psalm 23:5 (KJV):

Thou preparest a table before me in the presence of mine enemies…

While many celebrate freedom in our land, the truth is that there is no lasting freedom where people refuse to resist sin. Sin is bondage. Sin causes oppression. People who talk about freedom and do not passionately strive to overcome sin in their own lives and in their community are deceived and oppressed.

There can be no rest until we are free from the power of sin and from slavery to the devil.

It is not enough that the Lord gives us rest.

> Come unto me, all *ye* that labour and are heavy laden, and I will give you rest. (Matt. 11:28, KJV)

God brought all of the children of Israel out of slavery in Egypt. God gave them liberty with little or no effort required on their part. Yet many did not enter into the Promised Land because of unbelief. In other words, they did not choose the liberty God gave them. They resisted God when it came time to go into the Promised Land because they saw they would have to fight for it.

When Moses went up into the mountain to talk with God, these people made an idol and started planning to go back to Egypt. Why? Because those you liberate still must will to be free as much as you will for them to be free.

The giants are huge. The odds are against us. The devil controls the media, the government, the military, the big businesses, the education system and even many churches and denominations in our country. Still, with God our ultimate victory is sure. We must win souls, make disciples, vote, get educated, grow big businesses, grow big churches, serve in public office, and we must pass our vision and resolve from generation to generation. Most importantly, we must resist sin and temptation with the grace of God. We must fight.

> But Jeroboam caused an ambushment to come about behind them: so they were before Judah, and the ambushment *was* behind them. And when

> Judah looked back, behold, the battle *was* before and behind: and they cried unto the LORD, and the priests sounded with the trumpets. Then the men of Judah gave a shout: and as the men of Judah shouted, it came to pass, that God smote Jeroboam and all Israel before Abijah and Judah. And the children of Israel fled before Judah: and God delivered them into their hand. (2 Chron. 13:13–16, KJV)

Once when the nation of Israel was split, the wicked northern nation of Israel came to attack the southern tribe of Judah. Israel surrounded Judah. But when the men of Judah saw they were surrounded and hopelessly outnumbered, they shouted to the Lord, and God delivered them from the schemes of their enemies.

Today, as we praise God, pray in faith, and obey His voice, God is going to deliver Satan and all of his forces into our hand!

Because of His mercy, God is sending revival again to America. This revival will not just touch homeless or confused youths in the streets and on college campuses; this revival will also impact other major facets of life and leadership in our nation.

Dr. Cindy Jacobs discusses what it's going to take to revive America. I highly recommend her book *The Reformation*

Manifesto—Your Part in God's Plan to Change Nations Today. Here are some excerpts of what she has to say:

"How do we see the kingdom of God come into every aspect of society? What would it look like if God's wisdom and righteousness were incorporated into our laws, government, educational systems, as well as into our workplaces, homes, and everything we do?"[10]

"In the past I believed that when the gospel of salvation was preached in my city, it would change the fabric of society as well. I believed there is a correlation between the numbers of believers in a city and the godliness of government and culture in that city. For example, in a city with a large number of believers, poverty and corruption should be the exception and not the rule.

But as God was teaching me this, I began to wonder about my own city. I live in the Dallas/Fort Worth metroplex area of Texas. I know for a fact that Dallas/Fort Worth has a reputation as a densely Christian city. So does Colorado Springs, where our ministry was located before we moved back to our home area in Dallas. However, both areas have poor sections, and their city governments struggle with the same moral issues as most other U.S. cities of their size. Though largely Christian, these areas are still not discipled and taught of the Lord.

Why is this? What is wrong?

It would seem that the number of Christians who live in an area should change the spiritual climate of that area, but I didn't have to look far before I saw that simply wasn't the case. Why is that? I think the answer lies in two main areas: (1) perhaps we as believers have not seen kingdom living and building as our role or (2) if we have, we don't know how to practically use biblical principles to change our cities into places where the will of God flows freely."[11]

"Simply put, we must establish God's kingdom according to His divine rule in each sector of society by dethroning the powers of darkness that hold the nations in their grip..."[12]

"There is an ongoing battle for authority over a region that won't be finally settled until we intercede or Jesus returns and casts Satan and his minions into the lake of fire. We need to pray that God's kingdom authority will be established over our nations. Of course, regions will not be free once and for all from Satan's attacks until Jesus returns. Each generation needs to watch and pray over their own generation."[13]

In a book by Dr. Lance Wallnau I read the story of a divinely orchestrated meeting between Loren Cunningham, the founder of Youth with a Mission, and Bill Bright, the founder of CRU (Campus Crusade for Christ). In 1975 Cunningham was praying and God showed him a strategy for turning the world around for Jesus Christ. This strategy focused on seven areas: Church, Family, Education, Government and Law, Media, Arts, entertainment, sports, and Commerce, science, and technology.

The next day, Loren Cunningham had a meeting with Dr, Bill Bright. Dr. Bright shared with him how God had identified areas to concentrate on to turn nations to Christ. They were the same areas the Lord had shone to Loren Cunningham, with slightly different wording.

Loren Cunningham called them "mind molders." Bill Bright called them "world kingdoms." Dr. Lance Wallnau relates this story in his book, *Invading Babylon*. Dr. Wallnau calls these spheres of cultural influence "seven mountains."[14]

He writes, "I sensed the Lord telling me, 'He who can take these montains can take the harvest of nations.'"[15]

Dr. Wallnau goes on to say, "In order to take the seven mountains of culture for Christ's Kingdom, we must understand the interaction between the Church, the Gospel, and the culture.[16]

"When we think that the Church Mountain is the only spiritual mountain, we form a great divide between the Church and culture. We imply that the Church is the holy spiritual mountain and the rest of the mountains are of the world and profane.

"The shocking truth is that each mountain is a spiritual mountain! The devil's skill in leading us to think differently has resulted in the spiritual invasion of foreign deities into every area once held by followers of Christ. As we surrendered our colleges and universities, the intellectual seducing spirits of false enlightenment took the hippies of the 1960s and made them the professors who teach your children in college today! This invasion is all the more ironic when you consider that the first 230 colleges and universities established in the United States were planted for the education and development of Christians, ministers in particular. This secular-sacred split has made the Church Mountain almost entirely irrelevant to society today.[17]

"The truth is that all nations are already being discipled through the belief systems of those occupying their high places, the peak institutions of a nation's mind molders. If the Church leaves a vacuum by failing to occupy these high places with the teaching of the Kingdom, the enemy will seek to disciple the nations by building strongholds of deception that are guarded and advanced through those decision makers who rise to the top of the seven mountains of culture."[18]

It seems clear to many people that God is preparing believers in America for a revival that will not only focus on getting people into heaven, but it will also focus on welcoming heaven with all its virtue and glory into the earth. With this revival, we will finish what our Founding Fathers started. Rather than being a revival that lasts thirty or forty years and then fizzles out, it will be a revival that lasts until Jesus returns.

This revival will involve passing the vision of "God's Kingdom on earth" from fathers and mothers to sons and daughters. It will involve purposefully living to allow the Holy Spirit to mold the minds of future generations for Christ. It will involve purposefully living to allow the Holy Spirit to not only save us, but educate us and use us to shape policies that conform to the teachings of the Bible, policies in law, government, education, business, and every facet of culture.

This revival will restore American sovereignty under God, bring America's industries back from foreign shores, and rebuild America's cities. It will bring back American ingenuity and progress. It will bring the solutions for injustice and cures for incurable diseases. It will unite people across racial and cultural divides. Americans from all backgrounds are going to spread the Gospel, save the nation, and put the devil under our feet. Then together, we are going to share with the nations of the world, not spreading colas, burgers, pornography, computers, and mobile phones, but spreading the Gospel of God's love, which is the solution to every human problem we face on earth. This is the day for liberty.

11

God Our Supernatural Deliverer

Two of my favorite Old Testament prefigures of Christ are Jonathan and David. Jonathan was the son and heir-apparent of Saul, the first King of Israel. Jonathan died fighting Israel's enemies with his father, which made way for David to become the second king of Israel.

When they first met Jonathan and David became close friends because of what they had in common. Both men possessed an extraordinary faith in the God of Israel and His ability to deliver people.

The Philistines oppressed the people of Israel during the days of Saul's reign. Jonathan would raid the garrisons of the Philistines and bring war on the people. One day Jonathan challenged the young man that carried his armor to go with him on a daring attack on the Philistines.

> Then Jonathan said to the young man who bore his armor, "Come, let us go over to the garrison of these uncircumcised; it may be that the LORD will work for us. For nothing restrains the LORD from saving by many or by few." (1 Sam. 14:6, NKJV)

Jonathan and his armor bearer killed about twenty men before Saul's army came and finished the battle. And the Bible says, "So the LORD saved Israel that day, and the battle shifted to Beth Aven" (1 Sam. 14:23, NKJV).

I love the heart of Jonathan. He believed that nothing could restrain the God of Israel from saving and delivering His people, whether He had a lot of soldiers, or just two.

Many days later, the Philistines sent forth a champion, named Goliath, to challenge Saul and his whole army. Goliath taunted the men who were with Saul by the valley of Elah. David, a young shepherd boy heard the words of the Giant, and volunteered to go kill the Philistine warrior.

The giant laughed and cursed when he saw David come out to fight him.

I like what David said next.

> Then David said to the Philistine, "You come to me with a sword, with a spear, and with a javelin. But I come to you in the name of the LORD of hosts, the

> God of the armies of Israel, whom you have defied. This day the LORD will deliver you into my hand, and I will strike you and take your head from you. And this day I will give the carcasses of the camp of the Philistines to the birds of the air and the wild beasts of the earth, that all the earth may know that there is a God in Israel." (1 Sam. 17:45–46, NKJV)

And, yes, God delivered David out of the hand of the giant. And David cut off the giant's head.

David said, "This day the Lord will deliver you into my hand." That is so powerful to me! I believe that today is the day of salvation, the day of victory. With God, victory is not some day out in the future. Nor is it back in the past.

Whatever the battle, we cannot focus on the past or the future. We must concentrate on now. Faith is about the now. "Now faith is..." (Heb. 11:1, KJV)

Many a day I wake up and start to sing from Psalm 118:24, and within moments I am rejoicing!

> This *is* the day the LORD has made; We will rejoice and be glad in it. (Ps. 118:24, NKJV)

And then, let's think again about Jonathan's declaration: "For nothing restrains the LORD from saving by many or by few."

What faith these two men exhibited! Both Jonathan and David had great faith in the delivering power of God. They had been trained in the Torah. They had heard the marvelous stories of how God had faithfully delivered His people time and time again.

They heard how Abraham took his friends and his household servants, and delivered his nephew Lot and his family from four kings and their armies. They heard how the people of Israel had been slaves in Egypt for over four hundred years, and how God with one man, Moses, brought plague after plague on Egypt until the nation bowed its knee and let God's people go free.

They heard how God dried the waters of the Red Sea and the Jordan River so the children of Israel could cross on dry land.

They heard how Joshua and the people marched around the great walls of Jericho for seven days and then God caused the walls of that heathen city to fall. And they took Jericho.

They heard how God empowered Samson, one man, to kill a thousand Philistine warriors with just the jaw bone of an ass.

They heard how Gideon and God, with only three hundred men, defeated the armies of the Midianites, the Amalekites, and others from the east.

But Jonathan and David did not just hear these stories. They meditated on these stories. They thought about and sang about these stories. They believed these stories about the faithfulness of God. And whenever they got a chance, they stepped out. They took risk! They attacked! They put their trust in God and believed Him to use His power on their behalf.

Like the enemies had erected the walls of Jericho, Satan has erected great walls in our society to keep God out of people's lives. Today, it's time for these walls to fall.

The Bible makes it clear that we are in a spiritual war with spiritual forces in high places. Today in our country, the devil controls the institutions of cultural direction such as media, education, and government. Demons (rather than the Word of God) influence the executive branch, the judicial branch, and the legislative branch of our federal government. They control the democrats and the republicans. Those being influenced by these devils are working to dissolve our nation into tyranny using chaos, terror, and division. Out of the chaos they hope to replace our Christian America with some communistic, atheistic totalitarianism. How can we save our nation? The odds are against us. The challenges are overwhelming. The giants are fierce, and they are entrenched behind huge walls of money and power. But they will not succeed, because God is real.

Here's a question we need to ask: If Christians are reengaging in the political arena, and Christians are praying, why are our elected officials not turning our nation around for Jesus? Why is evil continuing to increase in our land? If God answers prayer, and so many are praying why don't things turn around?

> You ask and do not receive, because you ask amiss, that you may spend *it* on your pleasures. (James 4:3, NKJV)

Maybe we are asking amiss, when it comes to praying about our politics. We are in a spiritual war to save our world.

Satan got Adam and Eve to pursue the temptation for the forbidden tree. Even today, Satan tempts us with negative emotions to stir people to self-defeating actions.

Jesus did not fall for it. Although Satan tempted Him time and again, Jesus always resisted the devil and remained faithful to the Father's will.

Believers in America have been manipulated to vote out of fear, suspicion, and lust without knowing what the Father's will or plan is for America.

> Thy kingdom come. Thy will be done in earth, as *it is* in heaven. (Matt. 6:10, KJV)

Jesus told us to pray this way. I wonder if He wants us to vote this way. I wonder if He wants us to live this way. "Thy kingdom come. Thy will be done in earth, as *it is* in heaven."

> All nations whom thou hast made shall come and worship before thee, O Lord; and shall glorify thy name. (Ps. 86:9, KJV)

It is clear in many passages of scripture that God's will is for all nations to come to know Him so they can be blessed like Israel was.

Christians allow democrats and republicans, conservatives and liberals, to make promises that have nothing to do with the will of God; promises of personal wealth and comfort. We do not concentrate our financial support, or our prayer support on God's will, and we end up being maneuvered into voting for the "least evil candidate." Although we should all vote for the person who will be the best at bringing America to repentance and humility before the Lord God, year after year since the 1980s our voting power has been neutralized.

We cannot have lasting prosperity or freedom apart from the Kingdom of God and His righteousness.

Like Jonathan and David we have to hear and meditate on God's Word (the testimony of His faithfulness). We have to apply the Word, act on it as though we believe it is true. Through prayer, we need to go after all the power Jesus Christ makes available to His Church. We need to step out. And take risks! We need to go on the offensive, spreading the Gospel, buying property, running for office, leading businesses, supporting our churches, and raising our children with the vision of God's Kingdom on earth as it is in Heaven. We need to nominate, support, and elect only leaders who will turn America in repentance and obedience back to the Lord Jesus Christ. We need to put our trust in God and believe Him to use His supernatural power to deliver our nation.

God loves all nations. He loves our America. He has proven that nothing hinders Him from delivering people, no matter how overwhelming the odds may be against them. With faith in God the Body of Christ in America can take on the winner's mindset. As long as there is still one person who believes God, America can be saved. We may lose some battles, but ultimately we will be delivered, just like in the Bible. The tide is turning. The Church is Awakening. God is going to deliver the nations through His Church and put sin and evil under our feet.

12

The Gospel, the Church, and the World

God created His Church to win souls and teach people His Word. In other words, the local Church was created by God to make disciples for Christ's Kingdom.

The world's communities are made up of thousands of lost, disillusioned, and hurting people. Jesus came for the world. He came to heal, deliver, save, and restore people to the dignity and hope they were created for. Today, Jesus is looking for people who will let Him work through them.

Words are the key to restoration since lies were the key to our destruction. Adolf Hitler's strategy was: "If you tell a lie often enough people will believe it as the truth."

Satan is the father of lies. He is using lies to turn people away from God. The devil lied to Eve and took the world away from her and Adam when they believed the lie and sinned against God.

The only remedy for the curse that came upon the earth when Adam believed the lie is the Gospel Truth of Jesus Christ. (The Gospel is the good news of what God has done restoring humanity to the Kingdom of God through Jesus Christ.)

It is the work of the church to spread the Gospel and to help people grow into the likeness of Jesus Christ. Just as Jesus was faithful to the Heavenly Father and His Kingdom all the days of His life, so will be this new race of humans, born again by the same Holy Spirit that raised Jesus from the dead.

Every Christian has the ministry of continuously spreading the message of God's love in compelling ways throughout the community and the culture.

Together work to help people discover God and His love, discover their place in God's family (the local church), and discover their potential to do the works of Jesus Christ Himself throughout the community.

Notice what Jesus said in John 14:12–13 (KJV): Verily, verily, I say unto you, He that believeth on me, the works that I do shall he do also; and greater *works* than these shall he do; because I go unto my Father. And whatsoever ye shall ask in my name, that will I do, that the Father may be glorified in the Son.

The church family is the environment in which new believers grow in faith and love. As you hear the Word of God taught each week, attend classes and small group Bible studies, and as you serve together in the church, you will become more and more aware of God's presence. From the Bible you will learn how to receive power and instruction from the Throne of our Lord Jesus Himself. You will learn to focus your life on His purposes and bring His solutions to the earth's problems. And you will learn to increase your passionate love for God, for one another, for your city, for the nations, and for lost people.

The love of God will become real to the city through "Christ-like" disciples serving the community in Jesus's name. Our dream is that revival breaks out all over America. And that leaders from every facet of culture including business, government, education, and media will be committed Christians working to save our country.

America's democratic republic is the oldest lasting government in history. Of course, nothing is perfect, so some adjustments have been made as the nation has walked through history with God. However, in the days ahead, I believe that we might hear of those who want to totally alter America's constitution, giving more power to international organizations like the United Nations.

For many Christians, this will be a sign of the unavoidable dark times. They will continue to believe things are bad in the world because things are supposed to get worse in the last days, so there is nothing we can do to stop evil.

If we believe that the world is dark because it is supposed to be dark, then there is no hope and we cannot resist evil. But what if things are bad in the world because the human race has been enslaved? What if things are bad because mankind is sinful? If we understand that things are bad because mankind is enslaved to sin, then the Blood of Jesus gives us power to not only resist evil, but to overcome it. As Christians we have to keep believing that Jesus is our hope, and that things can be changed in our country and that the local church is indeed the hope of the world.

In the Old Testament there is the story of a young man named Joseph who God used to save his family and the nation where he lived from famine.

Joseph was sold into slavery by his brothers. Ten of his brothers were jealous of him because he was the favored son of their father Jacob. Even in Egyptian slavery, Joseph walked in great integrity and excellence before God.

Joseph faced many trials and landed in prison in this foreign land through no fault of his own. Yet even in prison he maintained his relationship with God, served his masters well, and was trusted and promoted for his faithfulness.

Eventually, through a series of events, Joseph rose to be second in command in the land of Egypt under Pharaoh, the King of Egypt himself. In his position Joseph was able to advise Pharaoh in a plan that saved the entire nation from death in a seven-year famine that came. God's plan was to use Joseph to supernaturally save his family and the nation where they were all living.

What caused Joseph to be in position to save the nation of Egypt? I believe it was his willingness to serve whoever was over him and to make them successful. In other words, Joseph did not let his negative circumstances keep him from loving people. (Joseph foreshadowed what Jesus would do for humanity, and what His Church will do today.) Joseph forgave the brothers who had sold him, the people who enslaved him, the woman who had lied on him, the fellow prisoner who forgot about him, the Pharaoh who oppressed him. Joseph kept serving people faithfully for God.

At home Joseph had learned faithfulness. In Egypt he served his masters as he had served his father.

I believe that Joseph helps us to see something very important for God's last days church. Lost people around us will be filled with terror in the days to come. They will be doing everything they can to save their families and their businesses from the horrors that are coming upon our nation. Because they do not know how to connect to God, they will not have a clue how to fix America's problems. As Christians walk with God in simple service, on their jobs and in their communities, lost people will come to look to them for solutions that work (they may not know where you got those great ideas!). Like Joseph brought God's counsel to Pharaoh, so I believe the church will bring God's solutions to our communities.

Because of the sins in our nation, darkness is spreading. The curse is bringing social upheaval, natural disasters, broken homes, and bankrupt cities. Leaders are looking for answers, but they are not looking to God. They do not have access to the supernatural wisdom that comes from the Presence of the Holy Spirit. God wants us to experience His presence in the church culture, and then to carry His presence out to heal our communities, and save the lost like Jesus did.

I believe that God wants believers to serve the ungodly leaders where ever we work, and to help them successfully overcome the curse attacking their businesses, departments, schools, homes, and neighborhoods. Our job is to bring the ideas, the integrity, the excellence, and the creativity of Heaven into the confusion and corruption of this world and turn back the curse in Jesus's name. That's the work of the Church in the earth. We are to pray that people in authority will be won to Christ as they see the love, honor, integrity, and excellence with which we serve them. Wherever we are employed, Christians are to serve with God's faith, hope, and miracle working power in order to help our nation overcome the things that are coming.

To do this we have to love everybody like our Lord Jesus loves them. We cannot be angry with them. We may face a period of persecution or ridicule. But we have to love eve-

ryone. Pray for them. We must be so loyal, so faithful, and so excellent in our work that they eventually trust us with their biggest unsolved problems. And like in the case of Joseph, God will give us the solutions that will bring our nation through the night with a light from above.

This is a new way of thinking for many of us. I must admit that it was difficult for me to accept at first. I was used to thinking in terms of "taking over for Christ!" But the devil turned the tide against Christianity in this country. Many unbelievers in positions of authority have been convinced that Christianity is "the threat." We can no longer play into their paranoia by exhibiting a "takeover mindset."

On the other hand, everyone is struggling to find solutions to the world's problems, and everyone is looking for faithful and loyal employees. Jesus has already taken over. When it comes to people, the Lord has brought us to the Kingdom not to take over, but so we can serve like He showed us. If we serve people for their benefit, then perhaps they will see the love and the supremacy of Jesus Christ through our integrity, loyalty, and excellence, and perhaps they will come to Him.

We will work together until this revival spreads to all the nations of the world; until economic problems, race problems, crime problems, poverty problems, energy problems, social justice problems, family problems, all problems, have Heavenly solutions, and every nation comes out of

the darkness of sin into the light of God's blessing through Jesus Christ. Jesus gave us God's vision for the world in the Lord's prayer: "Thy Kingdom come. Thy will be done on earth as it is in Heaven." Together, let us work diligently toward that day.

13

The First Word and the Last

Let us therefore come boldly unto the throne of grace, that we may obtain mercy, and find grace to help in time of need.

—Hebrews 4:16 (KJV)

The purpose of the Cross was to bring mankind to the Throne. The Bible makes it clear that each individual is saved by grace through faith (Ephesians 2:8).

Grace comes from the Throne of God. His throne is identified as the Throne of Grace because God dispenses mercy to undeserving people who simply put their faith in Jesus as their Lord and Savior.

The Old Testament picture of this is found in the Ark of the Covenant, which God told Moses to make. It was a box covered with gold where the presence of God would be among the tribes of Israel. Inside the box was the law, the commandments God expected His people to keep. The Mercy Seat, on the top of the box was where the Presence of God rested.

The Mercy Seat represented the Heavenly reality of God's Throne of Grace from which His mercy flows freely through the Lord Jesus Christ.

Jesus Christ is the firstborn from the dead. Some theologians might think that Peter, John, James or Paul was the first born again person, but according to the scriptures, it was Jesus himself.

> And he is the head of the body, the church: who is the beginning, **the firstborn from the dead** [emphasis mine]; that in all things he might have the preeminence. (Col. 1:18, KJV)

> For whom he did foreknow, he also did predestinate to be conformed to the image of his Son, that he might be **the firstborn among** [emphasis mine] many brethren. (Rom. 8:29, KJV)

When He rose from the dead, Jesus Christ became the first "born again" man. Likewise, we were all dead in our trespasses and sins (Eph. 2:1). When we surrender to Jesus as Lord and King of Heaven and Earth, we receive forgiveness of sins and a new nature. We are instantly born again on the inside by the same power that raised Jesus from the dead.

First John 4:17 says, "As he is so are we in this world."

When you get born again your spirit man on the inside is just like Jesus who is on the Throne. This is an amazing fact.

On top of this, the Lord Jesus promised that when He took the Throne, he would send back the Holy Spirit, the Presence of God Himself, to abide with us and empower us to do the miracles Jesus did and more (John 14:12–17). With all of this the Bible says, "Ye are of God, little children, and have overcome them: because greater is he that is in you, than he that is in the world" (1 John 4:4, KJV)

Is it really possible that the devil could ultimately defeat God's people? The problem is not on God's part. The problem, I believe, is that we need to grow in faith, to believe all the Bible says Jesus has done for us. We need to allow the Holy Spirit to grow us into the new identity Christ has made available to us. Like our Resurrected Lord, we are new creatures.

> Therefore if any man be in Christ, he is a new creature: old things are passed away; behold, all things are become new. (2 Cor. 5:17, KJV)

One of the most important jobs of the Church is to help people get born again and grow up into who God says they are.

I struggle to find the words to describe for people the stages of spiritual growth. I want to suggest five stages of spiritual development: Desire, Submission, Trust, Commitment, and Faithfulness. Whatever terminology we use, the end result of spiritual growth is to become faithful to God, like our Lord Jesus Christ.

The reason the earth is in the mess it is in is not because the devil is destined to take over the world. (His destiny is the lake of fire!) The reason the earth is messed up is because the people of God have yet to allow God to use them to the fullest of their potential in Christ. We must allow the Lord to develop faithfulness in us.

When Satan deceived the first Adam, the human race fell from the throne of God into slavery under sin.

Originally made in the image and likeness of God to rule and dominate the earth for God, man was Lucifer's worst nightmare. Mankind was given charge of the earth, to keep it from evil. But Adam forsook his responsibility to protect the earth when he ate of the forbidden tree.

Remember when Jesus was on earth, and he came from the river after being baptized by John, and the Holy Ghost came upon him? Then the devil tempted him to forsake his responsibility by disobeying God.

Satan wanted to make Jesus disobey God—leave His post—and forsake His responsibility as Lord protector of the earth.

Jesus is the only man Satan could not get to sin against the Father. Satan was able to get other human beings, like Adam, to forsake their duty, for some temptation like power, sex, money, fame, or to save their life.

> But Christ is faithful as a Son over God's house. And we are God's house if we keep on being very sure about our great hope. (Hebrews 3:6, NCV)

> And after He had appeared in human form, He abased and humbled Himself [still further] and carried His obedience to the extreme of death, even the death of the cross! (Phil. 2:8, AMP)

The point of the Gospel is that God was not willing to reign without us. Jesus came down the earth to raise us up to reign with Him from the Throne of David in Heaven (Eph. 2:5–6).

It was not enough for Jesus to defeat the devil. God wanted the human race to experience defeating the devil, who had defeated us. We were created as the guardians of the planet. We were created in the image and likeness of God. We were created the sons of God. We were created to subdue evil for God, here on our planet. We failed. We fell. We were captured as a race by our demonic enemies.

That is why God put the new humanity (the new creation) *in* Christ Jesus. We were placed in Him so that we could experience every victory He experienced (2 Cor. 5:17).

> And I will put enmity between thee and the woman, and between thy seed and her seed; it shall bruise thy head, and thou shalt bruise his heel. (Gen. 3:15, KJV)

After the fall and capture of humanity, God promised that the seed of the woman would one day rise again and put the devil under his foot. God has made the new human race *in* Christ and called us the Body of Christ so that we could experience putting the devil (putting evil), under our feet.

> For it became him, for whom are all things, and by whom are all things, in bringing many sons unto glory, to make the captain of their salvation perfect through sufferings. (Heb. 2:10, KJV)

God's purpose was not to bring the human race to Heaven in shame and defeat, but to bring us to Heaven with victory.

> Husbands, love your wives, even as Christ also loved the church, and gave himself for it; that he might sanctify and cleanse it with the washing of water by the word, that he might present it to himself a glorious church, not having spot, or wrinkle, or any such thing; but that it should be holy and without blemish. (Eph. 5:25–27, KJV)

God did this because of God's great love for mankind, also because His Word never returns to Him void. In the beginning God said, "Let us make man in our image, after our likeness: and let them have dominion over the fish of the sea, and over the fowl of the air, and over the cattle, and over all the earth, and over every creeping thing that creepeth upon the earth" (Gen. 1:26).

The plan of salvation was about even more than Jesus defeating the devil and making a way for people into Heaven. It was about bringing many people to heaven with glory. It was about restoring human beings to the righteousness, the dignity, the authority, the victory God created us for.

That's why I say the purpose of the cross was to raise humanity back up to the Throne which we were created for. Through Adam we have all tasted the agony of defeat, generations of suffering. Now in these last days, through Jesus, mankind is destined to taste the thrill of victory over evil, over sickness and plagues, over economic problems, over poverty, over sex trafficking, over child abuse, over war, over the flesh, and over all the works of the devil!

> To him that overcometh will I grant to sit with me in my throne, even as I also overcame, and am set down with my Father in his throne. (Rev. 3:21, KJV)

I personally believe that Heaven will be an eternal victory party! We will forever celebrate how the Lord Jesus Christ, our Heavenly Father, and the Holy Spirit gave us the victories we were created for.

So, let's go fight the devil, every day. We may not win every battle. We are not perfect. We don't have to be perfect to win this war. Jesus was perfect for us! Let's just keep growing in grace and faith. Even when we fall down, let's rely on the grace of Jesus and let Him lift us back up again and again.

Let's allow the Holy Spirit to grow us into faithful sons and daughters who overcome temptations and walk humbly with God. Let's fight to get every person saved, healed, and delivered with the Good News of what Jesus has done for the human race.

Let's build great churches, great schools, and great businesses. Let's rebuild our cities until everyone knows again that America is a wonderful Christian nation. Let us pray, give, serve, and make disciples until every nation is blessed through the Gospel and through the Lordship of Jesus Christ. Together, let's put the devil under His feet.

14
Conclusion

Verily, verily, I say unto you, He that believeth on me, the works that I do shall he do also; and greater works than these shall he do; because I go unto my Father.

—John 14:12 (KJV)

I believe that the greater works Jesus spoke of are before us today. What is it that Jesus Christ did not do? He is leading us to disciple the nations and to bring the blessings of Heaven upon all races and people groups.

Through His crucifixion, resurrection, and ascension to the throne of God, Jesus made all of this available to those who would follow Him.

God started by creating Israel as the model nation of what it means to be liberated and blessed by God. America and other Gentile nations are following the Messiah of Israel (Jesus) into the same freedom and blessing. This was prophesied in Isaiah 42:6, Isaiah 49:6, Luke 2:32, and Acts 15:15–17.

Every born again believer is a member of the new human race in Christ Jesus (2 Cor. 5:17). And we are destined to defeat evil in our nation, and carry the will of God, the Gospel of Heaven's salvation, to every nation, until nation after nation is free and blessed like God's model nation Israel was under King David and his son, Solomon, and the kingdoms of this world have become the kingdoms of our Lord and of His Christ (Rev. 11:15).

> After this manner therefore pray ye: Our Father which art in heaven, Hallowed be thy name. Thy kingdom come. Thy will be done in earth, as *it is* in heaven.... (Matt. 6:9–10, KJV)

NOTES

1. Andy Andrews, *How Do You Kill 11 Million People?* (Thomas Nelson Publishing, 2011), 39–40.
2. Dr. Vic Reasoner, *The Hope of a Christian World: Wesleyan Eschatology and Cultural Transformation* (The Aarminian Magazine Issue 1 Spring 2007 Volume 25), 1–4. www.fwponline.cc/v25n1/The%20Hope%20of%20 a%20ChristianWorld.html.
3. Stephen Douglas Wilson, *FIRST-PERSON: WWI's impact on Christians* (Baptist Press, Aug. 07, 2014. Copyright (c) 2014 Southern Baptist Convention, Baptist Press www.BPNews.net) http://townhall.com/news/religion/2014/08/07/ firstperson-wwis-impact-on-christians-n1876193
4. Ibid.
5. Greg L. Bahnsen, *The Prima Facie Acceptability of Postmillennialism* (The Journal of Christian Reconstruction, Vol. III, No. 2, Winter, 1976-77,

Covenant Media). www.cmfnow.com/articles/pt031.html.

6. American Banks Funded the Nazis, http://www.globalresearch.ca/american-banks-funded-the-nazis/31983.
7. Dr. Jeffrey A. Baker, *Cheque Mate, The Game of Princes* (Whitaker House, 1993), 63–64
8. Ibid. 67.
9. Ibid. 96.
10. Dr. Cindy Jacobs, *The Reformation Manifesto—Your Part in God's Plan to Change Nations Today* (Bethany House Publishers, 2008), 68.
11. Ibid. 69, 70.
12. Ibid. 187.
13. Ibid. 187, 188.
14. Lance Wallnau and Bill Johnson, *Invading Babylon—The 7 Mountain Mandate* (Destiny Image Books, 2013), 53–54.
15. Ibid. 54.
16. Ibid. 55.
17. Ibid. 63.
18. Ibid. 63, 64.

PERSONAL NOTES

Personal Notes

Our Heritage

Personal Notes

Personal Notes

CPSIA information can be obtained
at www.ICGtesting.com
Printed in the USA
FFOW05n1353301016